First World War
and Army of Occupation
War Diary
France, Belgium and Germany

41 DIVISION
Divisional Troops
Royal Army Service Corps
Divisional Train (296, 297, 298, 299 Companies ASC)
1 July 1916 - 30 April 1919

WO95/2631/2

The Naval & Military Press Ltd
www.nmarchive.com
Published in association with The National Archives

Published by

The Naval & Military Press Ltd

Unit 10 Ridgewood Industrial Park,

Uckfield, East Sussex,

TN22 5QE England

Tel: +44 (0) 1825 749494

www.naval-military-press.com

www.nmarchive.com

This diary has been reprinted in facsimile from the original. Any imperfections are inevitably reproduced and the quality may fall short of modern type and cartographic standards.

© Crown Copyright
Images reproduced by permission of The National Archives, London, England, 2015.

Contents

Document type	Place/Title	Date From	Date To
Miscellaneous Heading	WO95/2631/2 41 Div. S.S.O 41 Div S.S.O. 1916 July 1919 Apr In Italy Nov 17-Feb 18		
War Diary	La Creche	01/07/1916	20/07/1916
War Diary	Steenwerck	21/07/1916	17/08/1916
War Diary	Steenwerck	01/08/1916	17/08/1916
War Diary	Caestre	18/08/1916	23/08/1916
War Diary	Long	24/08/1916	31/08/1916
War Diary	Caestre	18/08/1916	23/08/1916
War Diary	Long	24/08/1916	05/09/1916
War Diary	Buire	06/09/1916	10/09/1916
War Diary	Bellevue Farm	11/09/1916	18/09/1916
War Diary	Buire	19/09/1916	02/10/1916
War Diary	Becordel	03/10/1916	04/10/1916
War Diary	E.11. Central	05/10/1916	11/10/1916
War Diary	Buire	12/10/1916	16/10/1916
War Diary	Longpre	17/10/1916	18/10/1916
War Diary	Fletre	19/10/1916	23/10/1916
War Diary	Reninghelst	24/10/1916	30/04/1917
War Diary	Sheet 28. J.34 d Central	01/05/1917	22/06/1917
War Diary	M. 4. Cent.	23/06/1917	30/06/1917
War Diary	Sheet 27 X 15 d.5.7.	01/07/1917	22/07/1917
War Diary	Boeschepe	23/07/1917	24/07/1917
War Diary	Westoutre	25/07/1917	14/08/1917
War Diary	Meteren.	15/08/1917	20/08/1917
War Diary	Wizernes	21/08/1917	15/09/1917
War Diary	G.35.c.3.5	16/09/1917	23/09/1917
War Diary	Caestre	24/09/1917	26/09/1917
War Diary	La. Panne	27/09/1917	06/10/1917
War Diary	St Idesbalde	07/10/1917	29/10/1917
War Diary	40 Rue De Liege Rosendael	30/10/1917	31/10/1917
War Diary	Camposampiero	01/03/1918	04/03/1918
War Diary	Lucheux	05/03/1918	20/03/1918
War Diary	Bresle	21/03/1918	21/03/1918
War Diary	Achiet-Le-Petit.	22/03/1918	24/03/1918
War Diary	Bienvillers Au Bois	25/03/1918	25/03/1918
War Diary	Bailleulval	26/03/1918	27/03/1918
War Diary	Gombremetz	28/03/1918	28/03/1918
War Diary	Authie	29/03/1918	01/04/1918
War Diary	Halloy	02/04/1918	02/04/1918
War Diary	Steenvoorde	03/04/1918	09/04/1918
War Diary	Sheet 28. G.4a.3.0	10/04/1918	27/04/1918
War Diary	Sheet 27 F 21 d 1.2	28/04/1918	14/05/1918
War Diary	La Lovie Chateau Sheet 27-Field. 49	15/05/1918	03/06/1918
War Diary	Nieurlet (nr. St Omer)	04/06/1918	06/06/1918
War Diary	Eperlecques	07/06/1918	25/06/1918
War Diary	Oudezeele.	26/06/1918	01/07/1918
War Diary	Sheet 27 K.21 b. 8.5.	02/07/1918	28/08/1918
War Diary	Wizernes	29/08/1918	02/09/1918
War Diary	K.24.A. 9.8	03/09/1918	26/09/1918

War Diary	Dallington Camp Sh. 27 L 29 C 8.2	27/09/1918	27/09/1918
War Diary	Sh. 28 G.23 b.8.4 (Domenern Camp)	28/09/1918	03/10/1918
War Diary	Sh. 28/1.26.c.8.3 (Lankhof Camp)	04/10/1918	16/10/1918
War Diary	Dadizeele	17/10/1918	19/10/1918
War Diary	Sh. 29/G 14 C 6.3	20/10/1918	20/10/1918
War Diary	Bisseghem	21/10/1918	28/10/1918
War Diary	Courtrai. (N2b 3.8)	29/10/1918	31/10/1918
War Diary	Courtrai (29/N 2b3 8)	01/11/1918	01/11/1918
War Diary	Sweveghem (29/O 1 a 6.5)	02/11/1918	04/11/1918
War Diary	Esscher (29/32b1.1)	05/11/1918	06/11/1918
War Diary	Sh. 29/1.9.b.7.2.	07/11/1918	09/11/1918
War Diary	Sh. 29/J 27d.9.1	10/11/1918	10/11/1918
War Diary	Sh. 30/M. 14d.9.1	11/11/1918	13/11/1918
War Diary	Nederbrakel Billet 86	14/11/1918	17/11/1918
War Diary	Billet No 1. Sant Bergen	18/11/1918	21/11/1918
War Diary	27 Adamstraat Grammont.	22/11/1918	11/12/1918
War Diary	Enghien	12/12/1918	12/12/1918
War Diary	Hal	13/12/1918	13/12/1918
War Diary	Braine L'Alleud	14/12/1918	16/12/1918
War Diary	Marbais. (106 Rue de Priesmont)	17/12/1918	17/12/1918
War Diary	Mazy	18/12/1918	18/12/1918
War Diary	Waret la Chaussee	19/12/1918	19/12/1918
War Diary	Huy	20/12/1918	10/01/1919
War Diary	Marienburg 5 Bayented Central Cologne.	11/01/1919	30/04/1919

WO95/2631/2

41 Div. S.S.O

BEF

41 DIV

S.S.O.

1916 JULY - 1919 APR

IN ITALY NOV 17 - FEB 18

Army Form C. 2118.

WAR DIARY
or
INTELLIGENCE SUMMARY
(Erase heading not required.)

Instructions regarding War Diaries and Intelligence Summaries are contained in F. S. Regs., Part II. and the Staff Manual respectively. Title Pages will be prepared in manuscript.

Place	Date	Hour	Summary of Events and Information	Remarks and references to Appendices
LA CRECHE	1-7-16		Capt P.W. PROCKTER relieved MAJOR E.F.T. TRAILL as S.S.O. Refitting to mend. Visited H.Qrs of and Brigade.	
"	2.7.16		"	
"	3.7.16		"	
"	4.7.16		" Empty petrol tins now being collected & conveyed by D.S.C. to nearest point in connection with the water supply for the troops in the forward lines	
"	5.7.16		Refitting to mend.	
"	6.7.16		Lieut H.M. MORRIS relieved Capt E.S. ROBINSON no S.O. 122 Infantry Brigade. Capt E.S. ROBINSON admitted to Hospital	
"	7.7.16		Refitting to mend.	
"	8.7.16		"	
"	9.7.16		"	
"	10.7.16		"	
"	11.7.16		Supplies drawn from STEENWERCK station by Train longues at 6 A.M. Refitting of dumps taking place at 10 A.M. for one day only. Refitting to mend. Visited H.Q. of and Brigade.	
"	12.7.16		"	
"	13.7.16		"	
"	14.7.16		"	
"	15.7.16		"	
"	16.7.16		"	
"	17.7.16		"	
"	18.7.16		Demount stores dump started. Visited H.Qr of and Brigade	
"	19.7.16		"	
"	20.7.16		"	

Army Form C. 2118.

WAR DIARY
or
INTELLIGENCE SUMMARY
(Erase heading not required.)

Instructions regarding War Diaries and Intelligence Summaries are contained in F. S. Regs., Part II. and the Staff Manual respectively. Title Pages will be prepared in manuscript.

Place	Date	Hour	Summary of Events and Information	Remarks and references to Appendices
Stanwerck	21/7/16		Refitting as usual	
"	22/7/16		do	
"	23/7/16		do	
"	24/7/16		do Visited H.Qs of Brigades.	
"	25/7/16		do	
"	26/7/16		do The supply of patrols from the Army Reserve Field Park hitherto was made to rank orders of I Corps.	
"	27/7/16		do do	
"	28/7/16		do Supply of pollution from Base renewed	
"	29/7/16		do do	
"	30/7/16		do do	
"	31/7/16		do Visited H.Qs Brigades.	

C. Grant Napier
Lt Col Comdg
11 Divn

2449 Wt. W14957/M90 750,000 1/16 J.B.C. & A. Forms/C.2118/12.

Army Form C. 2118.

WAR DIARY
or
INTELLIGENCE SUMMARY
(Erase heading not required.)

Instructions regarding War Diaries and Intelligence Summaries are contained in F. S. Regs., Part II. and the Staff Manual respectively. Title Pages will be prepared in manuscript.

Place	Date	Hour	Summary of Events and Information	Remarks and references to Appendices
STEENWERCK	AUGUST			
"	1		Supplies continue to be drawn from railhead by Train wagons at 7 AM and delivered to the Dumps, refilling taking place from 8.30 to 10. am.	
"	2		Refilling as usual. Second crop of green clover now obtainable.	
"	3		Refilling as usual	
"	4		do	
"	5		do	
"	6		do	
"	7		Visited H.Q. and Brigades	
"	8		do	
"	9		do	
"	10		do	
"	11		do	
"	12		do	
"	13		do	
"	14		Orders received to send Brigades for rest under new scheme	
"	15		do	
"	16		122 Bde move to Caestre. 23rd Div commence to relieve 41 Div	
"	17		Train H.Q. move to Flêtre. 122 Bde Transport Caestre. 123 Bde move to Thelies	

2449 Wt. W14957/M90 750,000 1/16 J.B.C. & A. Forms/C.2118/12.

Army Form C. 2118.

WAR DIARY
or
INTELLIGENCE SUMMARY
(Erase heading not required.)

Instructions regarding War Diaries and Intelligence Summaries are contained in F. S. Regs., Part II. and the Staff Manual respectively. Title Pages will be prepared in manuscript.

Place	Date	Hour	Summary of Events and Information	Remarks and references to Appendices
TZANEEN AUGUST.	1		Supplies continue to be drawn from Pietersburg. Trains leaves at 7 AM and arrives at its destination taking take 5-30 to 6:30 hrs Returning it arrives. Becomes one of grass eaten was out holes	
	2		Rest day in Camp	
			Units H.Q. and Brigades	
			Forts. Victoria reached. Pietersburg left Artillery reached.	
			a 123 POR 34 POR 6 Cos 23rd Div. remount dep at	
			Pietersburg 122 POR or or from Camp	

2449 Wt. W14957/M90 750,000 1/16 J.B.C. & A. Forms/C.2118/12.

Army Form C. 2118.

WAR DIARY
or
INTELLIGENCE SUMMARY
(Erase heading not required.)

Place	Date	Hour	Summary of Events and Information	Remarks and references to Appendices
Caestre	Aug 18		Railhead changed from Steenwerck to Caestre. Corps troops handed over to 23rd Div.	
"	19		23rd Div. 124 Mob. mur to Hooke Boom.	
"	20		Refilling as usual. Gave Dépôt at Steenwerck handed over to 23rd Div. Div. troops mun to FLETRE. Scherpenberg (Belown) Tram slip returned to Railhead STEENWERCK.	
"	21		S.T.O. departs by road to AMIENS and motoring from D.H.Q. Capt LADD acting as S.S.O.	
"	22		Two cheap returns noted to troops entraining 23rd Aug. (Pouran)	
"	23		34th Division in extenso for ABBEVILLE - PONT REMY + LONGPRÉ Two cheap returns issued to troops entraining 24th inst. (Pouran)	
LONG.	24		Remainder of Division entrains.	
"	25		Returns shown from VIGNACOURT by 3rd D.S.C. All Artillery & D.A.C. now fed by S.S. Div Troops. Troops concentrating in the vicinity. Hostiles see Anyone H.Q.s	
"	26		123 Bde. Train west of troops arriving.	
"	27		Refilling as usual	
"	28		do	
"	29		do	
"	30		do	
"	31		do. 6 lorries issued for animals.	

S.S. 41st Div.

Instructions regarding War Diaries and Intelligence Summaries are contained in F. S. Regs., Part II. and the Staff Manual respectively. Title Pages will be prepared in manuscript.

WAR DIARY
or
INTELLIGENCE SUMMARY

(Erase heading not required.)

Army Form C. 2118.

Place	Date	Hour	Summary of Events and Information	Remarks and references to Appendices
Caestre	18		23rd Div. 724 [illegible] move to Nord [illegible]. Caestre. Corps troops handed over to	
	19		Refilling as usual. Coal Depot at Steenwerck handed over to 23rd Div	
	20		Div troops move to FLETRE. Salvage [illegible] (balance) & [illegible] stock returned to Railhead STEENWERCK.	
	21		S.S.O. departs by road to AMIENS under instructions from D.H.Q. Capt LADD acting as S.S.O.	
	22		Two days rations issued to troops entraining 23rd [illegible] (Preserved)	
	23		Half Division entrain for ABBEVILLE. PONT REMY & LONGPRE. Two days rations issued to troops entraining 24th [illegible] (Preserved)	
LONG.	24		Remainder of Division entrain. Rations drawn from VIGNACOURT by 17th Div. S.C.	
	25		ALL Artillery & D.A.C. now fed by S.S. Div Troops they being [illegible] in the valley. [illegible] all Brigade H.Q.s. 123 Bde feeds rest of Cointreau [illegible].	
	26.		Refilling as usual.	
	27		do	
	28		do	
	29		do :- Clover issued for animals.	
	30		do do	
	31		do do	[illegible] S.S.O. 41 Div

Army Form C.2118

Vol 5

41 Div Train

WAR DIARY
or
INTELLIGENCE SUMMARY
(Erase heading not required.)

Instructions regarding War Diaries and Intelligence Summaries are contained in F. S. Regs., Part II. and the Staff Manual respectively. Title Pages will be prepared in manuscript.

Place	Date 1916	Hour	Summary of Events and Information	Remarks and references to Appendices
LONG	Sept 1		H.Q. Train with Divisional Artillery to D.A.C. train for Doreau Refilling as usual. Div Artillery to feed by Supply Col at the front Col.	
"	2		do	
"	3		do	
"	4		Refill in morning rations in afternoon for Brigades moving. Refilling as usual for 124 Bde. H.Q. train 122 & 123 Bdes transport sent for	
"	5		forward area to which place rations are sent by Supply Column.	
DAIRE	6		Railhead changes to ALBERT 122 123 Bdes & Infantry entrain for forward area.	
"	7		Transport of 124 Bde forward by road to forward area	
"	8		Refilling as usual	
"	9		do	
"	10		do	
"	11		do for Div troops, 122 & 124 Bdes. 123 Bde refill at FRICOURT returns same	
BELLEVUE FARM	12		do for Div Troops ALBERT by light railway	
"	13		Sent them from ALBERT by light railway	
"	14		Div Artillery D.A.C. refill near BELLEVUE FARM & the 3 Infantry Bdes at FRICOURT.	
"	15		Refilling as usual	
"	16		"	
"	17		"	
"	18		Division Except Artillery moves back to rest area	

Army Form C. 2118.

WAR DIARY
or
INTELLIGENCE SUMMARY
(Erase heading not required.)

Instructions regarding War Diaries and Intelligence Summaries are contained in F. S. Regs., Part II. and the Staff Manual respectively. Title Pages will be prepared in manuscript.

Place	Date 1916	Hour	Summary of Events and Information	Remarks and references to Appendices
BUIRE	Sept 19		Refilling bombs for whole Division moved to BUIRE - DERNANCOURT Road	
"	20		Refilling as usual	
"	21		"	
"	22		"	
"	23		Divisional troops in attack sent refill at BECORDEL.	
"	24		Refilling as usual	
"	25		"	
"	26		"	
"	27		123 Brigade refill at Becordel	
"	28		Refilling as usual.	
"	29		Refilling as usual	
"	30			

Capt W Rooter Capt
Comg D.3.m. Train
41st Divn

Army Form C. 2118.

WAR DIARY
or
INTELLIGENCE SUMMARY

(Erase heading not required.)

Instructions regarding War Diaries and Intelligence Summaries are contained in F. S. Regs., Part II. and the Staff Manual respectively. Title Pages will be prepared in manuscript.

Place	Date 1916	Hour	Summary of Events and Information	Remarks and references to Appendices
BUIRE	Oct 1		Refilling as usual. Winter scale of fuel now in force.	
"	2		Train H.Q. proceed to BECORDEL.	
BECORDEL	3		Refilling as usual	
"	4		Train H.Q. proceed to QUARRY E.H. cashier on ALBERT-BRAY road.	
E.H. Cashier	5		Refilling at BECORDEL as usual.	
"	6		do	
"	7		do	
"	8		do	
"	9		do	
"	10		do	
"	11		Train H.Q. now to BUIRE. No 2 bgy now to camp near DERNANCOURT and encamp with their Brigade. Refilling as usual. Major Pockets proceeds on leave and is relieved by Lieut H. S. Todd.	
BUIRE	12		Refilling as usual for Div. Troops at BECORDEL. No 3 & 4 bgys of Train now return to BUIRE and refit there.	
"	13		Refilling as usual. Railhead for Divn. including Hoy EDGE HILL. D Troop short of hay and some Brigade kept by Divn Transport.	
"	14			

WAR DIARY
INTELLIGENCE SUMMARY

Army Form C. 2118.

(Erase heading not required.)

Place	Date	Hour	Summary of Events and Information	Remarks and references to Appendices
BUIRE	15th Oct		Refitting as usual.	[initials]
BUIRE	16th		Demand arrived to have 15th bgde leave for 10th Corps area. (All Divnan except arty.) Transport proceed by Road. 124 Bde entrain this day while 122 & 123 Bdes entrain tomorrow. A.D. Div troops Divisional to draw extra 2/6 bacd for L.D. breaking stores.	[initials]
LONGPRÉ	17th		Divn Headquarters arrived at HALLENCOURT. Railhead changes VIGNACOURT. Railhead for Div troops is MERICOURT. Refitting	[initials]
LONGPRÉ	18th		Supply Column draws from VIGNACOURT as usual. In addition it obtains full 1 unit of Preserved Loaves for emergencies by Div during train journey. Refitting	[initials]
FLETRE	19th		S.S.O. proceeds from LONGPRÉ by road to FLETRE. Supply column draws after train at VIGNACOURT. 122 Bde returns and changes at HUCCHENVILLE while bivd carrying 2 Bdes returns to FLETRE and dug in their respective Bde Refitting in new area. 124 Bde returns changes at Renscourt. Railhead CAESTRE for new area.	[initials]
FLETRE	20th		Railhead NIPPENHOEK. A04 6 days for Railhead by horse transport in moving into forward area.	[initials]
FLETRE	21st		Refitting. 123 Bde returns changes as Reserve.	[initials]
FLETRE	22nd		Refitting. 123 Bde draws by horse transport as moving into forward area	[initials]
FLETRE	23rd		Refitting. 122 Bde returns drawn by Supply Column dumped as Reserve Bde dump Area Reserve Advr Depn over J.M. J.A.A.D. to the Div. Divn is town H.Q. moving from FLETRE to RENING HELST.	[initials]
RENINGHELST	24th		Refitting. 122 Bde draws by horse transport in moving into forward area Refitting 11-0am fr all.	[initials]
"	25th			[initials]
	26th		Refitting as usual	[initials]

Army Form C. 2118.

WAR DIARY
INTELLIGENCE SUMMARY
(Erase heading not required.)

Instructions regarding War Diaries and Intelligence Summaries are contained in F. S. Regs., Part II. and the Staff Manual respectively. Title Pages will be prepared in manuscript.

Place	Date	Hour	Summary of Events and Information	Remarks and references to Appendices
RÉNINGHELST	27.10.16		Nothing to record.	
do	28.10.16		Nothing to record. ½ ration butter – 1g bacon in lieu.	
do	29.10.16		Nothing to record.	
do	30.10.16		Nothing to record. 1100 hrs Ration drawn from CAESTRE.	
do	31.10.16		Nothing to record. Attended conference at Army Headquarters.	

J.B.M. Thompson Major
for S.S.O. 41st DIVISION.

WAR DIARY
INTELLIGENCE SUMMARY

Army Form C. 2118.

Place	Date	Hour	Summary of Events and Information	Remarks and references to Appendices
RENINGHELST	1.11.16		Normal circumstances. Feeding strength - Men 19683 Animals 5931. 3000 kilos purchased this day by R.O.S. in accordance with D.D.S. + S. of II Army expense vouchers.	O.F.
"	2.11.16		Normal circumstances. ½ ration Hotis en train - 1 ½ bacon in lieu ½ " bacon " - MXV in lieu ½ " cheese " - 2 oz fresh veg. in lieu 130 Iron Rations drawn + issued to 123rd Inf. Bde.	O.F.
"	3.11.16		Wire received from 10th Corps Q. - Hay ration to be reduced by 2 lbs. Hay sent from trades will be reduced by 6 lbs. Local purchase not to take place up to 4 lbs. for light horses and 7 lbs. for heavy horses. Change to take effect on pack trains leaving Railhead 5th Inst.	O.F.
"	4.11.16		Normal circumstances. Further grants of straw purchase. Feeding strength - Men 19436 Animals 5953. Small quantity of salvaged ration received from H.N. Div. Salvage Coy.	O.F.
"	5.11.16		Arine Dump station in view of reduction of hay anming Railhead. Armoured Riot Sec. Armd Railhead nr 6 lbs.	A.S.O. O.F.

Army Form C. 2118.

WAR DIARY
or
INTELLIGENCE SUMMARY
(Erase heading not required.)

Instructions regarding War Diaries and Intelligence Summaries are contained in F. S. Regs., Part II. and the Staff Manual respectively. Title Pages will be prepared in manuscript.

Place	Date	Hour	Summary of Events and Information	Remarks and references to Appendices
RENINGHELST.	6.11.16		Nothing to report. Feeding Strength :- Men 1934, Horses 5893.	
"	7.11.16		Normal circumstances. Weather very wet. Pea soup served to poor train.	
"	8.11.16		Normal circumstances. A.A.O. visits D.D.A.V.S. Second Army.	
	9.11.16		Refilling as usual. Further Purchases of Hay & Straw made.	
	10.11.16		Refilling as usual. 2 m/s Lt. Kerr proceeded to take up duty as Purchasing Officer to 2nd Army.	
	11.11.16		Conditions normal.	
	12.11.16		The Artillery of 4th & 13th Divisions commence to change billets from WIPPENHOEK upon their return to the Division.	
	13.11.16		Exchange of Quick-lime made by orders of D.H.Q.	
	14.11.16		The Artillery of 2nd Australian Division sent to area & billets upon their departure for another area.	

Army Form C. 2118.

WAR DIARY
or
INTELLIGENCE SUMMARY
(Erase heading not required.)

Instructions regarding War Diaries and Intelligence Summaries are contained in F. S. Regs., Part II. and the Staff Manual respectively. Title Pages will be prepared in manuscript.

Place	Date	Hour	Summary of Events and Information	Remarks and references to Appendices
RENINGHELST	15.11.16		Returns sent as usual. Stores being dumped for Divl. Works at dump.	App.
	16.11.16		New Div. interviewed re the whole Division. The Div. return on promotion at Works being carpeted as the organisation.	App.
	17.11.16		Refitting as usual.	App.
	18.11.16		Refitting as usual. Other issues for empty oil drums to be sent to R.E. work for conversion into heating stoves.	App.
	19.11.16		Conditions normal. Incidence of snow in Belgium forbidden.	App.
	20.11.16		Refitting as usual.	App.
	21.11.16		Commence on this unit refitting to take place direct from the train the unfavourable repairing points being no longer used. S.S.O. attends conference re transport question.	App.
	22.11.16		Refitting as before.	App.
	23.11.16		Stray mirror taken on Railhead – 17 horses in use during change :– Men 1473. Animals :– 6065.	App.
	24.11.16		Park train 3½ hrs. late. Weather fine.	App.

2449 Wt. W14957/M90 750,000 1/16 J.B.C. & A. Forms/C.2118/12.

Army Form C. 2118.

WAR DIARY
or
INTELLIGENCE SUMMARY

(Erase heading not required.)

Instructions regarding War Diaries and Intelligence Summaries are contained in F. S. Regs., Part II. and the Staff Manual respectively. Title Pages will be prepared in manuscript.

Place	Date	Hour	Summary of Events and Information	Remarks and references to Appendices
RENINGHELST	25.11.16		Ordinary routine. Pack train in its lines. No Regtl. Trains. Divl. train in lines.	O.F.
	26.11.16		Nothing to report	O.F.
	27.11.16		25% Magazine in lieu of trains arrived in Pack train. Still no Regl trains — Divl trains proceed per supply column issued for lindays consumption. Regs per trains in pack train and asked to units for Wednesdays consumption. The whole Divl train is now frozen now in advance. (This is contrary to the instructions to contain throughout the Divl train.) Attended brigade conf. J.O.C. Domain at LA CLYTTE and was ordered to practice flat country.	O.F.
	28.11.16		Pack train late. Still no regl trains — Divl train in lines thereof. Feeding strength — Men 1943 Animals 6057	O.F.
	29.11.16		Potato + Bacon wave at Railhead. Pack train into lines. 1st Indian Stores + Spares (from magazine) to Reserve received from Decau lorry Purchasing Officer. - A horse (?)	O.F.
	30.11.16		General Routine. Feeding Strength:- Men 1928 Animals 6010 Veterinary Divisional portable Diffed opened. No appt with absentee troops	O.F.

Geoffrey ?????
A.D.O. War Services Major

2449 Wt. W14957/M90 750,000 1/16 J.B.C. & A. Forms/C.2118/12.

WAR DIARY or INTELLIGENCE SUMMARY

Army Form C. 2118.

Place	Date	Hour	Summary of Events and Information	Remarks and references to Appendices
RENINGHELST	1/12/16		Normal Routine. Received wire from Purchasing Officer II Army "A" area to the effect that a further 8½ tons had been added to the terrain during storage - Then 190 at 7 Amiens 5839.	
	2/12/16		3 lb potatoes & pack train + 1 lb bread issued in lieu by Station. Weather very cold.	
	3/12/16		Pack train 6 horse trot. 1000 lb Rice withdrawn at Railhead, no other quantities were issued from supplies held by No 17 D.S.C. 2/Lt Hoff commences hf supervise Div. bread dump	
	4/12/16		Normal Routine. 25 lb Margarine issued in lieu of Butter.	
	5/12/16		Just trucks station arrive at RENINGHELST from STRAZEELE. Visited Divisional Rear station. 4½ tons hay received from Purchasing Officer II Army A area	
	6/12/16		Normal Routine. 1120 lb Rice withdrawn at Railhead, no other quantities were drawn from No 17 D.S.C. Dump. Very balance of supplies on hand.	
	7/12/16		Normal Routine. Bulk received from Railhead (rations taken in charge at 25 train altho' 40 tons supplied). 3 tons billeted bales received from IX Corps troops Supply Column G Mann.	

Army Form C. 2118.

WAR DIARY
or
INTELLIGENCE SUMMARY
(Erase heading not required.)

Instructions regarding War Diaries and Intelligence Summaries are contained in F. S. Regs., Part II. and the Staff Manual respectively. Title Pages will be prepared in manuscript.

Place	Date	Hour	Summary of Events and Information	Remarks and references to Appendices
RENINGHELST	8.12.16		Normal occurrences. Feeding strength Men — 15985 Animals 3642.	
	9.12.16		Special Routine. Visited A.I.O. 38th Div. and arranged to draw a guards Coy. supply train. Arrange to clear north in rear of Div. 7" from Murray Sid.	
	10.12.16		1 In lieu draw from I Corps supply Columns Dump, in consideration of X Corps because halting at Ham Personnel Dumps. To save south off-loading the were returned to S.W. Bath.	
	11.12.16		Normal routine. No road transport near POPERINGHE for Div. 7".	
	12.12.16		Normal routine. Loaner H.Q. R.A. & 1st Belgian R.A. commence to draw rations forage from Brigade Supply Dump in LOCRE (ROAD). Weekly feeding strengths of animals.	
	13.12.16		Drew train & Pack train in lieu of Motors.	
	14.12.16		To draw a Pack train for animals days. R.A.O. to withdraw from CAESTRE S.S.O. appointed venue of trains to Opens on arrival for troops Loose Dump	

2449 Wt. W14957/M90 750,000 1/16 J.B.C. & A. Forms/C.2118/12.

WAR DIARY or INTELLIGENCE SUMMARY

Army Form C. 2118.

(Erase heading not required.)

Place	Date	Hour	Summary of Events and Information	Remarks and references to Appendices
RENINGHELST	15.12.16		Ration Strength – 19687 Men – 5929 Animals. Park Strain 1 Oil tank Bread Issue in lieu Potatoes. As no supply can be drawn from 38th Divn (Div 7) owing to change of their R'head. Practice S.D.A.J. at Army Headquarters	P.F.
	16.12.16		Issued Rations Bread Issue in lieu Potatoes in Park Train	P.F.
	17.12.16		Nothing to report.	P.F.
	18.12.16		Attended Board (as President) to decide upon a suitable spot to form Corps Dore Dump. When weekly full train could be properly off-loaded. Proceeded to neck again turned Afternoon to formulate report. Practice X Corps Headquarters in re this matter.	P.F.
	19.12.16		Board re-assembled. Report drawn up and submitted to X Corps H.Q. 17 Inc. Maj. Staines received from Second Army Purchasing Officer A. Crea.	P.F.
	20.12.16		No Potatoes will arrive at Railhead in time for the position of same much to the regret of all Q.M.S. Some Bread re-issued this afternoon to re-imburse Rations implants made by me to G.O. in full coming at Railhead this night.	P.F.

Army Form C. 2118.

Instructions regarding War Diaries and Intelligence Summaries are contained in F.S. Regs., Part II. and the Staff Manual respectively. Title Pages will be prepared in manuscript.

WAR DIARY
INTELLIGENCE SUMMARY

Army Form C. 2118.

(Erase heading not required.)

Place	Date	Hour	Summary of Events and Information	Remarks and references to Appendices
RENINGHELST	21.12.16		Tractor Avenger — from 19185 Brigade 6027. Lord Brassey again assisted and three of proposed new units are from repr, now subjected to X th Corps Headquarters. Received instructions to evacuate present forage dump by 10.0 a.m 23rd.	P.R
	22.12.16		3½ D Train Ridding for new annex at Railhead. Instrs consignment to purchased to 000 lgr 8 Platoons at In 16.50. New scale of forage issue into vogue. Decide to commence removing reserve forage stored at 81.3 m Camp.	P.R
	23.12.16		Sent R.O. to DUNKIRQUE to purchase Paraffin. Plenty available but purchasers must supply the receptacles.	P.R
	24.12.16		Pack train slight loss. Same issued in lieu of picture.	P.R
	25.12.16		Xmas Day. Pack train halt.	P.R
	26.12.16		Nothing to report.	P.R
	27.12.16		Normal routine. H½ Ins Arrais & Hay received.	P.R

Army Form C. 2118.

WAR DIARY
INTELLIGENCE SUMMARY
(Erase heading not required.)

Instructions regarding War Diaries and Intelligence Summaries are contained in F. S. Regs., Part II. and the Staff Manual respectively. Title Pages will be prepared in manuscript.

Place	Date	Hour	Summary of Events and Information	Remarks and references to Appendices
RENINGHELST	28.12.16		Feeding strength – Men 19323 Animals 5940	Q.P.
	29.12.16		Any horses on Railhead at pleas rate of 6 lbs. 80 lbs supplementary forage will therefore be required nightly.	Q.P.
	30.12.16		Pack train late. Attended B.R.T. at M5 a 3.3 in re laying down a new coal dump	Q.P.
	31.12.16		Feeding strength. Men 19599 Animals 5976	Q.P.

[signature]

2449 Wt. W14957/M90 750,000 1/16 J.B.C. & A. Forms/C.2118/12.

Army Form C. 2118.

WAR DIARY
INTELLIGENCE SUMMARY
(Erase heading not required.)

Instructions regarding War Diaries and Intelligence Summaries are contained in F. S. Regs., Part II. and the Staff Manual respectively. Title Pages will be prepared in manuscript.

Place	Date	Hour	Summary of Events and Information	Remarks and references to Appendices
RENINGHELST	1.1.17		Issuing Strength Jan 1956.5 Animals 596.6. Pack Train 1 hr late. 10,000 Kilos straw received from N.Z. Div Train. 9½ tons Hay & Straw received for 2nd Army P.O.L.A. limber.	QP
	2.1.17		1½ th Bats running a train only balance to be drawn from below 1st supplies from No 2 D.S.A.D. received this train from Railhead. Visited DUNKIRQUE to settle paraffin question.	QP
	3.1.17		Second consignment of Iron Rations ammo at Railhead. First consignment of 7 Divisions in lieu of potatoes also arrived at Railhead. Visited D.D.S.A. "J." at Headquarters.	QP
	4.1.17		100 gals Paraffin drawn from Railhead, which normally will sell to issuing at ½ full.	QP
	5.1.17		Normal circumstances. During temporary absence of to bn during, assume command of train also for 4th Divisn.	QP
	6.1.17		Pack Train very late. Hay ammo at Railhead at 8 th. Owing to non-arrival of trucks no sufficient forage was available this day. No one full to the dump at G 32 habitual owing to Z to next dump at M 5 a 3.3	QP

WAR DIARY or INTELLIGENCE SUMMARY

Army Form C. 2118.

Place	Date	Hour	Summary of Events and Information	Remarks and references to Appendices
RENINGHELST	7.1.17		Today strength – Men 19879 Animals 5389. Issued our Forage suitable to supplement the Ration. Bulk Pack Trains trotting & nervous, browse (amongst fuel) at MS a. 3.3. 20½ tos Supplementary forage sent to Railhead also 8½ tos in Tractors	P.A.F. P.A.F.
	8.1.17			P.A.F.
	9.1.17		1¼ tos Maize received from 2nd Army Purchasing Board	P.A.F.
	10.1.17		Pack Train late. Horses A.Q. 1 122 + 124 Mules	P.A.F.
	11.1.17		Pack Train late again. Also Forage to Fforse stables the stable pulps corn & milk in line of corps	P.A.F.
	12.1.17		Pack Train 1 hour late. 17½ tos Supplementary forage received this day and dumped at KESTEEL MOLEN.	P.A.F.
	13.1.17		Pack Train arrives to time. Some stores coming from 2nd Army Purchasing Board. Weather very wet.	G.C.

Army Form C. 2118.

Instructions regarding War Diaries and Intelligence Summaries are contained in F. S. Regs., Part II. and the Staff Manual respectively. Title Pages will be prepared in manuscript.

(Erase heading not required.)

Army Form C. 2118.

WAR DIARY
or
INTELLIGENCE SUMMARY
(Erase heading not required.)

Place	Date	Hour	Summary of Events and Information	Remarks and references to Appendices
RENINGHELST	14.1.17		Draining strength Jun 14th 61 Annuals 5919. Received 8 before Xmas kept from R.A.O. Requested R.A.O. if Xmas boxes & Mails is lieu of Tea sent for the Devons.	
	15.1.17		S.J.'s Commence replying from Canada by 2, 3 & 4 boys respecting.	
	16.1.17		Issue some of boxes & Mails made to men in trenches.	
	17.1.17		60% That Mail cannon again to some at trailways Infy + awards in the rations was sent to canteen at Railway Dump of knowing Drew 18 box of both and 47th Devs. as I did not have any available.	
	18.1.17		Normal Routine. Further fall of snow.	
	19.1.17		Nothing to report.	
	20.1.17		Hour of Reputing changed — Men of Devons beginning first instant of 16th Devon Pack Travel very bad.	

Army Form C. 2118.

WAR DIARY or INTELLIGENCE SUMMARY

(Erase heading not required.)

Instructions regarding War Diaries and Intelligence Summaries are contained in F.S. Regs., Part II. and the Staff Manual respectively. Title Pages will be prepared in manuscript.

Place	Date	Hour	Summary of Events and Information	Remarks and references to Appendices
RENINGHELST	21.1.17		Feeding strength :- Men 19692 Animals 5902. "Hair Dressing" being taken.	QMS
	22.1.17		P.M. + Biscuits down for Railhead for Army Troops. Issue - 1 days' own rations now yesterday for Railhead, 1 ... day's issue for Supply Column + reserve Army. An hour and 12 days' fuel reserve.	QMS
	23.1.17		1/4 Rain of N.B.O. Still "frying." Issues as per MO 29 Prisoners of War &c.	QMS
	24.1.17		Pack train nearly 7 hours late. One day's extra oats issued "Horse Ration" to be issued tomorrow for Railhead.	QMS
	25.1.17		Wind producing Bread. It sends all further arrangements of Supply to RENINGHELST Junction of WIPPENHOEK.	QMS
	26.1.17		Pack train again very late. Sent Supply Officer Ohs Tync Machine Gunner in Supply System.	QMS

Army Form C. 2118.

WAR DIARY
or
INTELLIGENCE SUMMARY
(Erase heading not required.)

Instructions regarding War Diaries and Intelligence Summaries are contained in F. S. Regs., Part II. and the Staff Manual respectively. Title Pages will be prepared in manuscript.

Place	Date	Hour	Summary of Events and Information	Remarks and references to Appendices
RENINGHELST	27/1/17		Feeding strength Men – 20,350 Animals – 6189. Hay drawn at 10 tons. Ration train reached WIPPENHOEK at 3.40 p.m.	O.R.
	28/1/17		Ration train arrives 1.30 p.m. Ration trouble still continues.	O.R.
	29/1/17		No more of hay drawn from R.A.O. up to full scale, and one & I days Advance to front drawn from 47th Division & 15 In Arm'd for CAESTRE.	O.R.
	30.1.17		More Rations. Hay supplies and a dump to last until trains.	O.R.
	31.1.17		20 tons second further 20 expected from BRUAY. Feeding strength Men 20,654 Animals 6237. Needs daily issue	O.R.

Capt W. Richardson
R.O.

Army Form C. 2118.

WAR DIARY
INTELLIGENCE SUMMARY
(Erase heading not required.)

Instructions regarding War Diaries and Intelligence Summaries are contained in F. S. Regs., Part II. and the Staff Manual respectively. Title Pages will be prepared in manuscript.

Place	Date	Hour	Summary of Events and Information	Remarks and references to Appendices
RENINGHELST	1.2.17		Feeding strength :- Men 20,480. Animals 6312.	L.S.L.
	2.2.17		Pack train late. No gun or equipment issued.	L.S.L.
	3.2.17		Pack train again late. — ½ M.B.O. & W.P.O. Ins. grade biscuits. ½ Bacon in lieu ½ butter. Grain, vegetables fresh. hay frozen. (½ g bread issued) 65% P.M. 20% F. Meat. Stew "freezing".	L.S.L.
	4.2.17		Major Roberts proceeds to England on leave. Capt Lake to be acting S.A.O. during his absence.	L.S.L.
	5.2.17		Pack train late. 60% Forage train issue.	L.S.L.
	6.2.17		Pack train in on time. Biscuit in lieu of bread & Meat. Stew weather continues.	L.S.L.
	7.2.17		Attended conference held by Divisional Commander. Future bread ration to be varied.	L.S.L.

Army Form C. 2118.

WAR DIARY
INTELLIGENCE SUMMARY
(Erase heading not required.)

Instructions regarding War Diaries and Intelligence Summaries are contained in F.S. Regs., Part II. and the Staff Manual respectively. Title Pages will be prepared in manuscript.

Place	Date	Hour	Summary of Events and Information	Remarks and references to Appendices
RENINGHELST	8.2.17		Sunday. Strength Men. 196/8. Animals 620½. No stuff or other in stock to supplement Hay drawn from Railhead. Issued Army Purchase Ibs. rations accordingly.	E.S.L.
	9.2.17		Supplementary Forage arrived. Issued to reserve ration to No. 28 Prisoners of War Coy 5 pm. 5 to [?] maximum, as they were from the Area.	E.S.L.
	10.2.17		Pack horse my rest. Capt J.A. Leask (acting) A.A.O. indisposed — Corpl Wheeler "carrier on". "Issue" still general.	E.S.L.
	11.2.17		As per R.T.O. now on terms, two days ration to be received in 12th inst. Sugar "gear".	E.S.L.
	12.2.17		Drew 25 lbs Pressed Straw from Forage Barn at STRAZEELE in accordance with instructions from Presdt Army Purchasing Board.	E.S.L.
	13.2.17		Drew 10 lbs extra from A.A.O. NZ Division.	E.S.L.
	14.2.17		Usual Routine. Pack horse rest.	E.S.L.

2449 Wt. W14957/M90 750,000 1/16 J.B.C. & A. Forms/C.2118/12.

Army Form C. 2118.

WAR DIARY
INTELLIGENCE SUMMARY
(Erase heading not required.)

Instructions regarding War Diaries and Intelligence Summaries are contained in F. S. Regs., Part II and the Staff Manual respectively. Title Pages will be prepared in manuscript.

Place	Date	Hour	Summary of Events and Information	Remarks and references to Appendices
RENINGHELST	15.2.17		Training arranged. Ser. 1926/3. Arrivals 54401. Normal Routine.	L.S.R.
	16.2.17		Major P.D. Probert returns from leave. Drafts 20 Ors. Overseas from 55th Division.	Q.F
	17.2.17		Gas restrictions imposed. Pack train in to time.	Q.F
	18.2.17		Divine Day. "Gas restrictions". All fuel drafted by Horse Transport.	Q.F
	19.2.17		Normal Routine. ½ Ration Oats drawn from Railhead on no Hay delivery.	Q.F
	20.2.17		1 serviceable to feed 157/ R.S.A. again. Hour of Refilling changed to 10.0. a.m.	Q.F
	21.2.17		Normal Routine. Weather very wet.	Q.F

Army Form C. 2118.

WAR DIARY
INTELLIGENCE SUMMARY
(Erase heading not required.)

Instructions regarding War Diaries and Intelligence
Summaries are contained in F. S. Regs., Part II.
and the Staff Manual respectively. Title Pages
will be prepared in manuscript.

Place	Date	Hour	Summary of Events and Information	Remarks and references to Appendices
RENINGHELST	22.2.17		Feeding strength - Men. 19,659 Animals 5836. Normal Routine.	P.R.
	23.2.17		Today & until further notice only 30% Frozen Meat will arrive at Railhead - 55% Preserved Meat.	P.R.
	24.2.17		Normal Routine. Visited Second Army Headquarters.	P.R.
	25.2.17		No.1 Div. Supply Column ceases to operate for this Division at midnight. They are to be relieved by No.41 Div. Supply Column. See A.D. 1222 J.B. Chapeau reserve ration in forward area. Weather very mild.	P.R.
	26.2.17		Normal Routine. 9 two-tier wire received from STRAZEELE STORE.	P.R.
	27.2.17		60% Frozen Meat again arrives at Railhead. Issued weight of 10 x 80% the gross. Still weight of 10 the Fancy 819 the gross.	P.R.
	28.2.17		Feeding Strength. Men. 19,106 Animals 5859.	P.R.

[signature]
A.O. 41ST DIVISION.
MAJOR.

2449 Wt. W14957/M90 750,000 1/16 J.B.C. & A. Forms/C.2118/12.

Army Form C. 2118.

WAR DIARY
or
INTELLIGENCE SUMMARY
(Erase heading not required.)

Instructions regarding War Diaries and Intelligence Summaries are contained in F.S. Regs., Part II. and the Staff Manual respectively. Title Pages will be prepared in manuscript.

Place	Date	Hour	Summary of Events and Information	Weather	Remarks and references to Appendices
RENINGHELST	1-3-17		Fighting Strength. Men 18848. Horses 5381. Marched routine	Fine	P.J.S.
	2.3.17		30 feet 400 att ranks of E+F Railway Detachments (9th Corps) from 4 Div. attached to 216 A.T.C. for one week. Marched routine	Snow	P.J.S.
	3.3.17		Drew 10 tons charcoal from S.S.O. 57 Div weeks for 36, G 13 a.s.s.	Frosty	P.J.S.
	4.3.17		20 tons coal drawn from S.S.O. 3rd Aust. Div in motor lorries from D.A.D.S.T. 2nd Army	Bright	P.J.S.
	5.3.17		Marched routine. No curtain in bricklaying of am railhead	Snow	P.J.S.
	6.3.17		Changes over rail head to a range = 12 of feet keg.	Rain	P.J.S.
	7.3.17		Withdrawn at railhead 1058 tolens P.M. - relief withdrawn from Siding Point.	Windy	P.J.S.
	8.3.17		Call Horse 1½ hrs late. Arrangements made to relieve D.h. to remain dumps with 41 D.S.C. for 10 days thus leaving units without the usual 2 days meat. Note to Corps 0.5hr.	Snow	P.J.S.

2449 Wt. W14957/M90 750,000 1/16 J.B.C. & A. Forms/C.2118/12.

WAR DIARY or INTELLIGENCE SUMMARY

Army Form C. 2118.

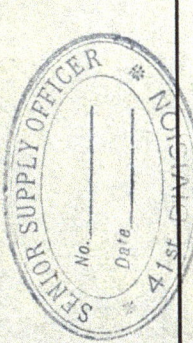

Place	Date	Hour	Summary of Events and Information	Weather	Remarks and references to Appendices
RENINGHELST	9.3.17		Fighting strength:- All ranks 1949 h. Animals 5317. 4 tin lorries have come in to Supply Section.	Dry Overcast	R.P.
	10.3.17		S.D.A.S. II Army visited Railhead at Reningles times. Usual Routine.	Mild	R.P.
	11.3.17		Major P.D. Probett indisposed. Capt L.A. Ladd "carries on". 10th Corps Q. issued (?) that 20,000 P.M. rations are now to Supply Column in accordance with instructions.	Biyer	R.P.
	12.3.17		Arranged with R.S.O. to cut off all bread issued to (in lieu of fresh vegetables) mess until notice, for Pack train.	Rain	R.P.
	13.3.17		It snows 10 tons bore from II Army troops Supply Column. Usual Routine.	Rain	R.P.
	14.3.17		8 tons bore drawn from II Army troop Supply Column. This Division to stand over & afford army for action to Supply train until further notice, at CAESTRE.	Rain	R.P.
	15.3.17		Paraffin sent round to various camps for lighting huts.	Fine	R.P.
	16.3.17		Usual Routine. Drew 120 tons Ration from Railhead.	Fine	R.P.
	17.3.17		Bread ration comes at Railhead today and until further notice at 25%, balance in biscuit. Fine.		R.P.

Army Form C. 2118.

WAR DIARY
or
INTELLIGENCE SUMMARY

(Erase heading not required.)

Instructions regarding War Diaries and Intelligence Summaries are contained in F. S. Regs., Part II. and the Staff Manual respectively. Title Pages will be prepared in manuscript.

Place	Date	Hour	Summary of Events and Information	Remarks and references to Appendices
KENINGHELST.	18.3.17		Training Singles". Then 2017 Annexes 511b. 4 Ind'd Fuldes have arrived in Supply area at R'head.	Dull.
	19.3.17		60% Bread on Pack Train. Lorries 20th inst. then Division commence to draw from Pack Train. Refilling will be at 8.0. am.	Dull + Windy
	20.3.17		60% Bread on Pack Train. Only 50% Frozen Meat will arrive Railhead on 20, 21 & 22.	Clear Warm
	21.3.17		Bread held on 200 th days 130 th Inf (expect part of Inf Ration withdrawn Supply Off Broad - to be distributed to supply for horse transport from train lines).	Fine
	22.3.17		Normal Routine.	Fall of Snow
	23.3.17		Only 22% Frozen Meat arrive Railhead. No fuel for this division to-day.	Fine
	24.3.17		No Frozen Meat. Preserved Meat in lieu. Hard Rations.	Fine
	25.3.17		60% Frozen Meat. Pack Train late.	Fine
	26.3.17		Pack Train very late. Aerodrome arrive at Railhead for Horse lines. Equivalent to Rations = 13 P.M.	Rain

Army Form C. 2118.

WAR DIARY
or
INTELLIGENCE SUMMARY
(Erase heading not required.)

Instructions regarding War Diaries and Intelligence Summaries are contained in F. S. Regs., Part II. and the Staff Manual respectively. Title Pages will be prepared in manuscript.

Place	Date	Hour	Summary of Events and Information	Weather	Remarks and references to Appendices
RENINGHELST	27.3.17		Ration Strength: Men.— 19474 Animals — 4525. Pack train very late. 4 ox sumer horse in supply section.	Fine	R.P.
	28.3.17		Pack train late. Her ox ration for stores the in relays to be arranged before the 29th inst. Necessary arrangements made at Reninghelst.	Zero	R.P.
	29.3.17		Pack train late. Normal routine.	Rain	R.P.
	30.3.17		Pack train came to time. Full movement in respect of New ox ration scheme for Reninghelst on 29th inst completed.	Fine	R.P.
	31.3.17		Pack train in to time. 19th Divsn Horses 10.T. total for the Div. Feeding Strength. Men.— 19509 Animals 4545.	Fair	R.P.

[signatures]

Army Form C. 2118.

WAR DIARY
or
INTELLIGENCE SUMMARY
(Erase heading not required.)

Instructions regarding War Diaries and Intelligence Summaries are contained in F. S. Regs., Part II. and the Staff Manual respectively. Title Pages will be prepared in manuscript.

Place	Date	Hour	Summary of Events and Information	Weather	Remarks and references to Appendices
RENINGHELST	1.4.17		Fighting Strength — Men - 1962, Animals - 4518. Normal Routine.	Showery	R.F.
	2.4.17		Reserve Ration in actuality held by 123 I. Bde. were inspected by Supply Officer of this Brigade, findings.	Dull	R.F.
	3.4.17		Normal occurrences	Heavy fall of snow	R.F.
	4.4.17		Normal Routine. Approximately 3000 kilos crushed Maize purchased from local ration.	Nil.	R.F.
	5.4.17		Normal Routine	Fine	R.F.
	6.4.17		123rd J. Bde. draw for Railhead for last time this morning, owing to their move from this area.	Fine	R.F.
	7.4.17		These ration reduced by no bay. 2 J. Bde will be reissued when available	Fine	R.F.
	8.4.17		Normal Routine	Fine	R.F.
	9.4.17		Horse Rations 190 Bde R.J.A. drawn for last time from WIPPEN HOEK owing to their migration from this area.	R'head showery	R.F.
	10.4.17		I received that 123 S. Bde. group will draw ration from WATTON on April 12th and subsequent days by horse transport.	fine	R.F.

2449 Wt. W14957/M90 750,000 1/16 J.B.C. & A. Forms/C.2118/12.

Army Form C. 2118.

WAR DIARY
INTELLIGENCE SUMMARY
(Erase heading not required.)

Instructions regarding War Diaries and Intelligence Summaries are contained in F. S. Regs., Part II and the Staff Manual respectively. Title Pages will be prepared in manuscript.

Place	Date	Hour	Summary of Events and Information	Weather	Remarks and references to Appendices
RENINGHELST	11.4.17		Feeding strength - Men 15635 Animals 4063 10 In Charge Men by 23rd Dec for the Divison.	Showery	P/C
	12.4.17		Normal Routine. R.O. proceeded to DUNKIRK to purchase Nut butter.	Dull & cloudy	P/C
	13.4.17		Normal Routine. One truck rations, one truck canteen comforts Railed for the Division.	Fair	P/C
	14.4.17		2/Lieut. [?] commenced to issue Railway stores in lieu bread, also Valises with some stores issued in lieu bread.	Fair	P/C
	15.4.17		Normal Routine.	Rain	P/C
	16.4.17		2/Lieut [?] has come as Railhead Supt. L.S. Load vans Reserve Rations initiated in lieu of present line [?] J 124 J Box.	Fine	P/C
	17.4.17		Normal Routine. Starting 16th inst 5 Ktre stores will be sent to stn S.W. corner S.D.S. J.II Army, [?]	S.W. Rain	P/C
	18.4.17		Normal Routine.	Rain	P/C
	19.4.17		Received from field trek of Inst Ryftans (came). Supply Actual leave tickets at Rhoads and reports [?] their respect.	Dull	P/C
	20.4.17		A.S.O. purchased 57 loaves bare gratings in ST OMER for 123 Box etc. Visited Depot Corps Headquarters D.D.D. & S Second Army [?] for period of 30 meetings to 17.3.1.D.	Fine	P/C

2449 Wt. W14957/M90 730,000 1/16 J.B.C. & A. Forms/C.2118/12. [?]

WAR DIARY / INTELLIGENCE SUMMARY

Army Form C. 2118.

Place	Date	Hour	Summary of Events and Information	Remarks and references to Appendices
RENINGHELST	21.4.17		Strength Details:- Men 14790. Animals 3540. H.Q., J.B.C. & R Batteries, 189 Bde R.F.A. drew rations to day and rations for A.S.G. 29th Div until the second echelon was sent. Further notice Purchase Branch asked to ship 2h day stores, owing to large arrivals of equipments, available.	O.R.
	22.4.17		Received 2 days rations from 2nd Corps Coy Purchase Branch. Moved 123 Inf. Bde. in training area at TILQUES.	O.R.
	23.4.17		Petrol Train 1 hour late. 2nd Platoon for man armoured drawn. Rations to be drawn tomorrow for NIPPENHOEK to replace drawn for Reserve Sup.	O.R.
	24.4.17		Note ration for H.D. drawn in full rate of 17th bring & reserves 2nd Platoon n. train.	O.R.
	25.4.17		123rd I.B. again drew ration for NIPPENHOEK. 2nd Platoon n. train.	Sale.
	26.4.17		Division to collect 1000 clean caps from him as arm on prisoners for II Army pursuant to order TERDEGHEM.	Free.
	27.4.17		On arrival of British (armoured) armoured R'd. alas 2nd Platoon. 122 Bde drew ration for horse lines for NIPPENHOEK. Rations & reserves ration will be drawn for VATTEN. The rules applies to 16/157 R.F.A.	Sale.
	28.4.17		1150 Petrol train arrived. X"" Corps Supply Column to be held in Reserve with others. Sent 2nd Platoon n. train.	Free.
	29.4.17		Usual Routine. 2nd Platoon n. train.	Free.

WAR DIARY

INTELLIGENCE SUMMARY

Army Form C. 2118.

Place	Date	Hour	Summary of Events and Information	Remarks and references to Appendices
RENINGHELST	30.4.17		Feeding strength Men 15250 Animals 3932. Hand Rations. Reserve Rations in forward area inspected by S.O. 123 Inf. Bde.	Weather Fine R.Q.

Army Form C. 2118.

WAR DIARY
or
INTELLIGENCE SUMMARY
(Erase heading not required.)

Instructions regarding War Diaries and Intelligence Summaries are contained in F. S. Regs., Part II. and the Staff Manual respectively. Title Pages will be prepared in manuscript.

Place	Date	Hour	Summary of Events and Information	Remarks and references to Appendices
Area 28 & 30 de ante	1.5.17		Feeding strength – Men 15225 Animals 3875. Animal scale (a) full scale rest regim this day	Fine. P.C.
	2.5.17		Feeding strength – Men 15275 Animals 3875. Horses & Ponies	Fine. P.C.
	3.5.17		Feeding strength – Men 15199 Animals 3874. Horses & Ponies	Fine. P.C.
	4.5.17		Feeding strength – Men 15209 Animals 3857. Some [?] forage recd at R'head	Fine. P.C.
	5.5.17		Feeding strength – Men 15517 Animals 3927. 26th Royal Fusiliers draw ration to-day for conveyance by 12D train Bn recd all round at ST OMER (previously to training area)	Fine. P.C.
	6.5.17		Feeding strength – Men 14517 Animals 3794. Small quantity of forage regarded rec morning R'head daily	Fine. P.C.
	7.5.17		Feeding strength – Men 14475 Animals 3773. Horse (122 J.) Bde in training area	Fine. P.C.
	8.5.17		Feeding strength – Men 14425 Animals 3795. Horses & Ponies	Fine. P.C.
	9.5.17		Feeding strength – 3838. 40 potato tubs now arriving for exchange 12th & presents & A mill re- join Division – require ration for exchange 12th & presents	Fine. P.C.

2449 Wt. W14957/M90 750,000 1/16 J.B.C. & A. Forms/C.2118/12.

WAR DIARY
INTELLIGENCE SUMMARY
(Erase heading not required.)

Army Form C. 2118.

Instructions regarding War Diaries and Intelligence Summaries are contained in F. S. Regs., Part II. and the Staff Manual respectively. Title Pages will be prepared in manuscript.

Place	Date	Hour	Summary of Events and Information	Remarks and references to Appendices
Steenvoorde	10.5.17		Feeding strength Men 14449 Animals 3817. Supply of sufficient hay drawn from Railway, no normans.	Fine
	11.5.17		Feeding strength Men 14172 Animals 4004. Issued on short further notice, ration to be raised to ordinary scale of 17th R.I.R. 16 Div. 26 J.R. & among hours in Div Area Rations (less rations) drawn 440 ordt boots K. Descriptions come in Pack train, of which 152 were petrol & accessory dressings.	Fine
	12.5.17		Feeding strength Men 15489 Animals 3998. General Rations.	Fine
	13.5.17		Feeding strength Men 15383 Animals 4024. Working party (9th 16th Div (9th R.I.R.)) drew ration for that time to-day for 41 Div. Tractors & Animals 65th Bde R.F.A. drew ration from the Divisions.	Fine
	14.5.17		Feeding strength Men 16414 Animals 5009. Vehicles 122 S.D. Bde in training area.	Fine
	15.5.17		Feeding strength Men 17708 Animals 5009. 73rd M.G. Coy. J. to be returned to the Division, strength 18th + horses (transferred). Horses return as reported by GSO 124 Bde.	Fine
	16.5.17		Feeding strength Men 20,946 Animals 5421. 124 Bde People draw 2 days ration returns, the present for mess. to training area. 122 Bde come to draw vagan for WIPPENHOEK this day.	Dull
	17.5.17		Feeding strength Men . Animals 5263. Issued rations for the 1st Transports + Parade.	Rain

Army Form C. 2118.

WAR DIARY
INTELLIGENCE SUMMARY
(Erase heading not required.)

Instructions regarding War Diaries and Intelligence Summaries are contained in F. S. Regs., Part II. and the Staff Manual respectively. Title Pages will be prepared in manuscript.

Place	Date	Hour	Summary of Events and Information	Weather	Remarks and references to Appendices
Sheet 28. S 34 d central	18.5.17		Feeding strength Men 19984 Animals 4572. 12th Inf. Bde. went to buy from WIPPENHOEK (by box car) with tr. srans. Ypres QUATTEN	Dull & Showery	P.R.
	19.5.17		Feeding Strength Men 16595 Animals 4714. 100 lb. Bread & Meat. also 9g. Potatoes issued by R.S.O.	Fine	P.R.
	20.5.17		Feeding Strength Men. 16664 Animals 4679. 11,000 Mens Rations stacked in local Dump in connection with forcing operations.	Fine	P.R.
	21.5.17		Feeding Strength Men. 16620 Animals 4692. Total 11,000 Mens Rations stacked in local Dump as for Yesterday. Now 124 J.Bde. to training area.	Dull & Heavy	P.R.
	22.5.17		Feeding Strength Men 16479 Animals 4849. Total 11,000 Mens Rations stacked in local Dump, making 33,000 in all. 72nd A.F.A. Bde. arrived to draw rations from this Division trains	Rain	P.R.
	23.5.17		Feeding Strength Men 17517 Animals 5691. Now Ration Stations	Fine	P.R.
	24.5.17		Feeding Strength Men. 17679 Animals 5798. Bags 20,000 pieces sleeping Iron & 8000 Sandbags Anti Aircraft - the latter to be taken. Railway trucks & packing RENINGHELST through Railway. Div Supply 6.30 am 122 J.Bde 6.30 am 123 J.Bde 7.0 am. Two strand(?) between 26th Bde R.F.A. (being) for mnfport 26th + rations. also 52nd Bde. R.F.A. & Special Brit Bef.(?) Bf. for mng(?) 27th + rations.	Fine	P.R.

Note first name of green forage

WAR DIARY

Army Form C. 2118.

Instructions regarding War Diaries and Intelligence Summaries are contained in F. S. Regs., Part II. and the Staff Manual respectively. Title Pages will be prepared in manuscript.

Place	Date	Hour	Summary of Events and Information		Remarks and references to Appendices
Sheet 28 G.3.d central	25.5.17		Feeding str. Nos. 19604 Animals 6484. Refilling took several men last two this morning towards 14 rain palais + petrol tin noted action below SW. Q 335/5	Jun.	Q.R.
	26.5.17		Feeding Str. Nos. 19569 Animals 7361 12 SDD OXO tyres	Jun.	Q.R.
	27.5.17		Feeding Str. Nos. 19744 Animals 7344 Sho Depart. to feed 277th A.F.A. Bde (Ohio A. Arty) for remaining 30 m + ussards also 73rd M.G. Bn for return fr 31st inclusive to.	Jun.	Q.R.
	28.5.17		Feeding Str. Nos. 19974 Animals 7505 A.O. J 122 J.B. inspected Shown Ration + Horses in forward area.	Jun.	Q.R.
	29.5.17		Feeding Str. Nos. 21.196. Animals 8237. Horses J forward.	Jun.	Q.R.
	30.5.17		Feeding Str. Nos. 21813 Animals 8295 March 124 Bn in training Area.	Jun.	Q.R.
	31.5.17		Feeding Str. Nos. 21710. Animals 8311. New Railhead this day + mustards – OUDERDOM	Jun.	Q.R.

Army Form C. 2118.

WAR DIARY
or
INTELLIGENCE SUMMARY
(Erase heading not required.)

Instructions regarding War Diaries and Intelligence Summaries are contained in F. S. Regs., Part II. and the Staff Manual respectively. Title Pages will be prepared in manuscript.

24

Place	Date	Hour	Summary of Events and Information	Remarks and references to Appendices
Shed 25 of 34 d central	1.6.17		Army Strength. Men 25293. Animals 8670. Four Other ranks late - arrived at rest Camp to join 64th Bn taken by. From 3rd not inclusive	Q.R.
	2.6.17		Army Strength. Men 25074. Animals 9952. Two Other Ranks (1st gun 19th Bn) taken 65 (gun carriages 1st & reserve) Routine round for first time	Q.R.
	3.6.17		Army Strength. Men 24950. Animals 8618. 216 A.T. 65 O.R.'s & 73 M.G. 65 armed with rations for last line taken. Some approx 20 lnc each forge for R.S.O. Pioneer + 10 lnc Decem. Zone from S.S.O. A7th Decem.	Q.R.F.
	4.6.17		Army Strength. Men 24896. Animals 8529. to ration Corps 1 X Bn supply troops (new)	Q.R.
	5.6.17		Army Strength. Men 18779 (due to reinforcements Y Arg) Animals 8521. Rasad Ridge	Q.R.C.
	6.6.17		Army Strength. Men 14501 (due to reinforcements Z Arg) Animals 8531.	Q.R.C.
	7.6.17		Army Strength. Men 20465 (due to reinforcements A. Arg) Animals 9625. From Gros Janction. + X Corps Brassier + 1st Supply H.F.C. Jealousy	Q.R.C.
	8.6.17		Army Strength. Men 23191 (due to reinforcements B. Arg) Animals 8643. World decade Any Headquarters	Q.R.C.

2449 Wt. W14957/M90 750,000 1/16 J.B.C. & A. Forms/C.2118/12.

WAR DIARY

INTELLIGENCE SUMMARY

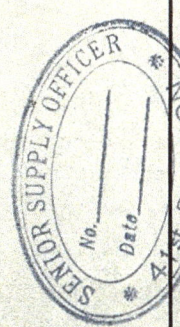

Army Form C. 2118.

Place	Date	Hour	Summary of Events and Information	Weather	Remarks and references to Appendices
Shew 28 3rd d area	9.6.17		Feeding Strength. Men 24311. Animals 8602. Rations + Gud - 13643 - to be maintained at Ration 12th - 13th - 14th	3 ins	Q.F.
	10.6.17		Feeding Strength - Men 24249 Animals 8608 Moved Rations	dull	Q.R.
	11.6.17		Feeding Strength. Men 22748. Animals 8566. To be held of 123 Bde. moved to 123 Bde depôt. no reserve	dull	Q.R
	12.6.17		Feeding strength Men 22608 (600 Rhodesians) Animals 8739. Sent one pack M.A.O. 1st Div. - 20 tn bale 20 tn oats the 7 tons delivered Nore Major Moline at Xth brigade Headquarters	fine	Q.R.
	13.6.17		Feeding Strength Men 22296 (7643 Rhodesians) Animals 9629. Moved Rations	fine	Q.R.
	14.6.17		Feeding Strength Men 26312 Animals 12269. Sent hay fodder + Bdoe artillery for 47th Div. 14th A.H.A Bde + 14, 96, 119 A.F.A. Bde most issued this morning - 123 + 124 J.B's at 8.30 am B.J. at 4 pm; refine at 7 am; 122, Ind J.B. at 5.0 am each	fine	Q.R.
	15.6.17		Feeding Strength Men 26530 Animals 12190. This division to feed 64th kam Inf (on 17th) and hay 111th kam Inf (on 16th)	fine	Q.R.

WAR DIARY
INTELLIGENCE SUMMARY
(Erase heading not required.)

Army Form C. 2118.

Place	Date	Hour	Summary of Events and Information	Weather	Remarks and references to Appendices
Sheet 28 F 34 d cent	16.6.17		Feeding Strength - Men 26678. Animals 12111. 24,000 Rd Stg Cobra in train. Borrowed van from Div Forge Dump to be returned later. Railhead trimmers and mill grain rations — WIPPENHOEK.	Fine	
	17.6.17		Feeding Strength. Men 26337. Animals 12064. Borrowed refilling supply train at 7.0 a.m. Issue ration at 2/1st A.F.A. Bde ff last time stamps	Fine	
	18.6.17		Feeding Strength Men 26054. Animals 12060. Drew Upon Supply train at 3.0 a.m. Ex Issued 193 Ratt Lg (Indian Army) for 20th entrance.	Fine	
	19.6.17		Feeding Strength. Men 24761. Animals 11427. All ration drawn from supply train at 3.0 a.m.	Rain	
	20.6.17		Feeding Strength. Men 25829. Animals 11459. Issue Indian Ratt time to 72nd A.F.A. Bde, who will be attached to pur by X the Corp. Supply Column.	Wet	
	21.6.17		Feeding Strength. Men 24811. Animals 10535. Issue grain Ratt last time to 86th A.F.A Bde who will attached to pur by X the Corps. Forage Supply Column. Is drew 30 tons fodder dump from R.A.O. RENINGHELST.	Fine	
	22.6.17		Feeding Strength. Men 24584. Animals 9717. bay dump at RENINGHELST – WESTOUTRE Road	Fine	

WAR DIARY / INTELLIGENCE SUMMARY

Army Form C. 2118.

Place	Date	Hour	Summary of Events and Information	Remarks and references to Appendices
M.4. Cent	23.6.17		Feeding Strength Men 24839 Animals 9717. Brig General H M.4 central	Fine
	24.6.17		Feeding Strength Men 24673 Animals 9687. Russell Russell - Swan column fot last line stores to 64th Lewis S.g.	Fine
	25.6.17		Feeding Strength Men 24473 Animals 9724. Philleigh Bridges and units front aside RENINGHELST road. Monte Army Headquarters	Fine
	26.6.17		Feeding Strength Men 23844 Animals 9656. Army of Repair - D.I.I. 5.0 A.M. 122 S/B 5.45 A.M. 123 S/B 6.15 A.M. 124 S/B 5.30 A.M. 119th A.T.F.A Bdl. first to hun of for stood ration Innocents the an drawn in CAESTRE Hdt A.T.A. Bde first ration stamps for last line - advancing posn by X th Bgsh D.A.4.	Dull & Stormy
	27.6.17		Feeding Strength Men 22379 Animals 8156. 64th A.S.F.A. Bde moved and ration for last line	Dull
	28.6.17		Feeding Strength Men 21031 Animals 6955. 122 S/B Bde gone to new area. Bulk food for long Convoys. Repling force X 3 c 1/2 2.	Fine
	29.6.17		Feeding Strength Men 21002 Animals 6923. Draw up load lim for RENINGHELST Railhead - Stores 4 Swans CAESTRE. 1000 left left behind being fed by S.S.O 47th Division (including Sw. Bus)	Fine
	30.6.17		Feeding Strength Men 11226 Animals 1677. 122 + 124 S/Brd repl in new area in RENING HELST - LA CLYTTE Road 123 J/B refln n Reserve at that cage.	Rain

Jumptulup Major
S.S.O.

WAR DIARY

INTELLIGENCE SUMMARY

Army Form C. 2118.

Place	Date	Hour	Summary of Events and Information	Weather	Remarks and references to Appendices
Sheet 27 X.15.d.s.7	1.7.19		Feeding Strength - Men 11169 Animals 1692. Train H.Q. move to new area (as per orders). Orders then received by 3 Bdes from at CAESTRE subsequent change in respective areas. Take over 42 Div BAC from S.S.O. 47 Div at EBBLINGHEM	Dull	R.F. R.F.
	2.7.19		Feeding Strength - Men 10198. Animals 1630. Open New Camp in NETEREN village	Fine	R.F.
	3.7.19		Feeding Strength - Men 10765 Animals 1623. Issue of laundry tickets at Hazebrouck - 126 IRS. 10.45 am 122 IRS. 11.0 am 123 IRS 11.15 am	Fine	R.F.
	4.7.19		Feeding Strength - Men 10640 Animals 1616. Moved Report. No. 23 T.M. Bde B.R.a. D.A.C. 157 Ade R.F.A. refill in their areas as before. 190 Ade R.F.A. continue to be fed by 47 Div	Fine	R.F.
	5.7.19		Feeding Strength - Men 10655 Animals 1620. Registry of Mules for feeding appears to have effect for is not increase. No 165 arrive in the area	Dull	R.F.
	6.7.19		Feeding Strength - Men 13150 Animals 3257. Div Staff return & be area for R.H. & Army and standard at A 26 a central when refilling takes place	Fine	R.F.

WAR DIARY or INTELLIGENCE SUMMARY

Army Form C. 2118.

Place	Date	Hour	Summary of Events and Information	Remarks and references to Appendices
Sheet 21 X.15.d.5.7	7.7.17		Feeding strength - Men 14,292 Animals 3360	QR
			190th Bde R. Fla draw rations on this area towards all units	QR
	8.7.17		Feeding strength - Men 14,230 Animals 4025	QR
			40% coffee ties packed at 7th & 8th further orders	
	9.7.17		Feeding strength - Men 14,229 Animals 4027	QR
			Visit Divisional Camp H.Q. Jas Deere 226 Tobby dinner rations for each man towards	QR Wed
			in the area - proceeding to LUMBRES for training	
	10.7.17		Feeding strength - 14,724 Animals 4061	QR
			Drew 20,500 K. hail ration from STEENBECK Railhead	
	11.7.17		Feeding strength - Men 15,385 Animals 4066. 19th Inland + 233 + 237 TMBys R.E. draw rations in	QR
			this area. Instruc'n for known sick to proceed with rations. 47th Divn 15th Stays relieving	
			in this area - rations to be drawn here towards for consumption 13th + onwards.	
	12.7.17		Feeding strength - Men 15,003 Animals 3916. Men Deere 225 76 bys R.E. rations to gas 233 76	QR
			by E.G. and with to rations by 47th Divn An Div. 15th + onwards. 32nd Royal Fusiliers proved to 7 Corps June	
			area. Known road will be drawn by 47th Divisn for an 15th + onwards.	

WAR DIARY
INTELLIGENCE SUMMARY
(Erase heading not required.)

Army Form C. 2118.

Place	Date	Hour	Summary of Events and Information	Remarks and references to Appendices
Sheet 27 X.15.a.5.7	13/7/17		Feeding Strength - Men 15790 Animals 3925. Near Renter	Nil
	14/7/17		Feeding Strength - Men 14,518 Animals 3864. Shops O.R.D. parcels arrived, on leave to England Except Army L.S. Lads with exception of Others	App L S L
	15/7/17		Feeding Strength - Men 14,830 Animals 3809. Normal Routine	Nil
	16/7/17		Feeding Strength - Men 14,725 Animals 3783. Normal Routine	L S L
	17/7/17		Feeding Strength - Men 14,630 Animals 3920. Div 50 Ins 1000 x 2 gals with 48h two tons each of X 60.A Sept 6.a. 10 x 60 A. hour lb. 10 x 60 A days Park and transports Rly not for 17 Div Arct 1700 (one reed session) 238 M.G. Co. some Regina robins for reserve farmers	Nil (Army) L.S.L.
	18/7/17		Feeding Strength - Men 14,802 Animals 3928. Area 7000 Rhins and sent up to forward area by but to accordance with instruction Amph there gate in charge. 12th Bn. are at NESTOUTRE area this note remain. 1 228 Fd Co now at forward area 12th Bn with be feed by any. Refilling Point M.21.0.8	L S L

WAR DIARY

INTELLIGENCE SUMMARY

(Erase heading not required.)

Place	Date	Hour	Summary of Events and Information	
Abeele	19.7.17		Feeding Strength - Men 14733 Animals 3924. R.P. Senders for 124 I.B. at CONQUEROR CAMP Vlamtge. M3 c D1.2. Convoys L.O. 124 Bde rode feed and water to of the Div. as have been fed by A.A.D. 47th Divn.	RP
XISdS.7	20.7.17		Feeding Strength - Men 17068 Animals 4393. Normal Routine	RP
	21.7.17		Feeding Strength - Men 17743 Animals 4505. 123 Bde now at WESTOUTRE area and will be fed by Army for CAESTRE by motors R.P. then M11 c.3.8	RP
	22.7.17		Feeding Strength - Men 17774 Animals 4374. 101&102 D.S. move to WESTOUTRE area. Feed Sub. Res. (102 102 have Bde) Senders their R.P. M5.c.29 Sum Ordnas 90 (Resd) orders for A.R.M. for Battle storaghel Regs & &	RP
BOESCHEPE	23.7.17		Feeding Strength - Men 17906 Animals 4245. H.Q. Div Sum move to BOESCH+EPE.	RP
	24.7.17		Feeding Strength - Men 17974 Animals 4309. Normal Routine	RP
WESTOUTRE	25.7.17		Feeding Strength - Men 23391 Animals 6026. Train R.O. now to WESTOUTRE. John Sub Res Balt from A.A.D. 47th Divn. Resumed charge to BRULOOZE	RP

WAR DIARY

Army Form C. 2118.

Instructions regarding War Diaries and Intelligence Summaries are contained in F.S. Regs., Part II. and the Staff Manual respectively. Title pages will be prepared in manuscript.

(Erase heading not required.)

Place	Date	Hour	Summary of Events and Information		Remarks and references to Appendices
WESTOUTRE	26.7.17		Issuing Sec. Rat. 28829 Animals 9479	Fine	P.W.F
			Road Ration		
	27.7.17		Feeding Sec. Rat. 24718 Animals 9437. Drew 5000 R. Sandbags through for haulage	Fine	P.W.F
			Major R.D. Roberts gassed in division the A.M.		
	28.7.17		Issuing Sec. Rat. 24556 Animals 9490	Fine	P.W.F
			Road Ration		
	29.7.17		Issuing Sec. Rat. 24610 Animals 9577	Wet	P.W.F
			Issue of Rum to 122 + 123 Bdes. Ft. arrangements being also made for carriage of Zrops		
	30.7.17		Feeding Sec. Rat. 24373 (less 6250 horses rations on Z day) Animals 9504	Wet	P.W.F
			Iron 24 hours and solid forage rations on 30.7. Forage Rations will serve as rations for the day		
			Bros. 5 MD J. Stretchers carried for X & 60 R. troops supply Column		
	31.7.17		Issuing Sec. Rat. Sec. 24588 (less 2100 horse rations on Z+1 day) Animals 6530.	D.W	P.W.F
			40 R Troops Arm Railway tops and Ind just force active		

Army Form C. 2118.

WAR DIARY
INTELLIGENCE SUMMARY
(Erase heading not required.)

Place	Date	Hour	Summary of Events and Information	Remarks and references to Appendices
WESTOUTRE	1.8.17		Feeding strs. Men 24430 Animals 9499. Issue of Rum made to whole Brigade.	P.R.
	2.8.17		Feeding strs. Men 24223 Animals 9452. Rations issued on free ration scale. Issue of Rum to Inf. Batns, Pioneers and R.E's &c.	P.R.
	3.8.17		Feeding str. Men 23977 Animals 9420. Issue of Rum to Inf. Batns, T.M.B's, M.G.Co, Pioneers R.E's.	P.R.
	4.8.17		Feeding str. Men 23396 Animals 9479. [illegible entries]	P.R.
	5.8.17		Feeding str. Men 23299 Animals 951 [illegible] (February 104 AFA Bde)	P.R.
	6.8.17		Feeding str. Men 22389 Animals 10786. [illegible]	P.R.
	7.8.17		Feeding str. Men 22774 Animals 10817. [illegible]	P.R.

WAR DIARY

INTELLIGENCE SUMMARY.

(Erase heading not required.)

Army Form C. 2118.

Place	Date	Hour	Summary of Events and Information	Remarks and references to Appendices
HESDOUVRE	8.8.17		Feeding etc 22972 Ancre 10742	See
			Issue rations for last time this day to 17th Div Bty	
	9.8.17		Issue etc Aisne 21107 Somme 9473	See
			Horses Running	
	10.8.17		Feeding etc Aisne 22663 Somme 9751	See
			4th Div D.A.C. Horse ration for last time for the Div this day. Started toward BRULOOZE	
			Issue of Rea. corn commenced to our Div Artillery during present reclined course	
	11.8.17		Feeding etc Aisne 19973 Ancre 7605	Wet
			Received (incl.firing) 10.0 am Ancre	
	12.8.17		Issue etc Aisne 19661 Ancre 7620	Fine
			123 3.B. rec'd to MEZEREN area send for meat last day & will be fed by us	
	13.8.17		Feeding etc Aisne 19606 Ancre 7397	Dull
			103 3.B. opening rations on X.9.a.3.7	
	14.8.17		Feeding etc Aisne 19373 Ancre 7569	Wet
			122 Bde rec to recce area. Started toward BAILLEUL	

WAR DIARY

INTELLIGENCE SUMMARY

Army Form C. 2118.

(Erase heading not required.)

Instructions regarding War Diaries and Intelligence Summaries are contained in F. S. Regs., Part II. and the Staff Manual respectively. Title pages will be prepared in manuscript.

Place	Date	Hour	Summary of Events and Information	Weather	Remarks and references to Appendices
METEREN	13.5.17		Strength ORs 13149		RKT
			Issue H.Q. and to METEREN	Wet	
			Issued the feed times from new stocks from R.A.O. 39th Div.		
	BERTHEN		Issued 122 & 3 G.C.R. to this area.		
	14.5.17		Strength ORs 13213 Animals 1906	Fine	RK
			Issued Rations		
	15.5.17		Strength ORs 13129 Animals 1841	Fine	RK
			88b Bread + 64 t forage meat		
	16.5.17		Strength men 13521 Animals 1875	Dull	RK
			Issued Rations		
	17.5.17		Strength men 13675 Animals 1866	Fine	RK
			Park Grave Vats		
	20.5.17		Strength men 13650 Animals 1572	Fine	RK
			125 + 123 S B on rest and re-org. for divers day training area Rations issued as by Army Order		
	28.5.17	LOZERINCS	Strength ORs - 122+123 SB - men 9214 Animals 1313 - 124 SB Men 4057 Animals 520	Fine	RK
			Supplies for 122 + 123 Bdes drawn from Relief Issue Store ST. OMER. Supplies for 124 Bde were drawn by Supply Officer 124 SB for BAILLEUL as the further action + their Bde Troops continue to draw from 39 DIV.		

Wt. W14422/M1160 350,000 12/16 D. D. & L. Forms/C/2118/14.

Army Form C. 2118.

WAR DIARY
INTELLIGENCE SUMMARY.
(Erase heading not required.)

Place	Date	Hour	Summary of Events and Information	Remarks and references to Appendices
WIZERNES	22.5.17		[illegible handwritten entries]	

WAR DIARY
INTELLIGENCE SUMMARY

Army Form C. 2118.

Place	Date	Hour	Summary of Events and Information	Remarks and references to Appendices
WIZERNES	29.8.17		Feeding sec. 122, 123, 124 Men. Men 13405 Animals 2253. Road Parties.	
	30.8.17		Feeding sec. 122, 123, 124 Men. Men 11995 Animals 2026. No 4 A.D.L.S. work party for Army & other forms out S1 OHER today 1045 to escort forward. 2 other work party [illegible] sent out. Men on the grade sick A Shelter on sideline.	
	31.8.17		Feeding sec. 122, 123, 124 Men. Men 12399 Animals 2041. Road Parties.	

WAR DIARY
INTELLIGENCE SUMMARY
(Erase heading not required.)

Army Form C. 2118.

Place	Date	Hour	Summary of Events and Information		Remarks and references to Appendices
WIZERNES	1.9.17		Feeding Nos. 122. 123. 124. SB. Men 12234 Animals 2019	Bull & Flour	Q.P
			Road Rations		
	2.9.17		Feeding do. 122. 123. 124. SB. Men 12304 Animals 2018	Am.	Q.P
			1 Gun 238 M.G. Coy. proceeded to relieve 1 Gun 123 M.G. Coy. nr ABEELE	Am.	
	3.9.17		Feeding do. 122. 123. 124. SB. Men 12377 Animals 2336 HQ 123 am to forward area		Q.P
			Road Rations		
	4.9.17		Feeding do. 122. 123. 124. SB. Animals 2076	Same	Q.P
			A.H.Q. HQ Coy moved nr Jun Pooln pp stn. 3 group trains. Road Rations		
			Rations n B⁰ & 7th men		
	5.9.17		Feeding do. 122. 123. 124. SB. Groups Men 12532 Animals 1992	Same	Q.P
			A.H.L. Coy. I S.B.G. & Pdr & I.T.A. moved & 21st Div area. Rations arr. ex a 5" + 6" am to Gp. Sgnl		
			4x 2" Am pt your tn to 7th men		
	6.9.17		Feeding do. 122. 123. 124 SB Groups Men 11762 Animals 1851	Same	Q.P
			Horses to various units dealt by diff Bhens in accordance with D.A.T. Helg Paris W.S. 17		
	7.9.17		Feeding do. 122. 123. 124. SB. groups Men 12302 Animals 1517	Same	Q.P
			Road Rations		

WAR DIARY
INTELLIGENCE SUMMARY.
(Erase heading not required.)

Army Form C. 2118.

Place	Date	Hour	Summary of Events and Information		Remarks and references to Appendices
WIZERNES	8.9.17		Testing Set. 122, 123, 124. SB Group. Ann. 1196. Answer 1194	Test	O.R
			23rd Probable matte to fire been. Rifle too raid for cond. 9th + 10th used. B.R.Q. show aim to be faulty.		
			Return for the Bust will be sent by Lamp filament to RENINGHELST for ex. 10th mor. DR consult		
			these but links note to record with ration by 8.0. Ties N.L. of Smoyst		
			Normal A 238 M.G 60 aim to fire acc Ration for Ann. 10th + Messages to be dam from Hy Rattan		
9.9.17		Testing No. 122, 123, 124 SB Group. Ann. 10th 2 Answer 1292	Test	Q/R
			None Strating		
	10.9.17		Testing Sets. 122, 123, 124. SB Group. Ann. 12860 Answer 1357		Q.R
			HQ + 3 Gun 139 SB Gr. formed to Novo at M.D.5. An anything associated as by CYLIE Marigot		
			focus a 10th + Alam Answer a 11th by the test mater for a. a.o. 39th N. to cam 12th Group		
	11.9.17		Testing Set. 122, 123, 124 SB Group. Ann. 10535 Answer 1292	Test	Q.R
			as feel 109 Rifles. R.I.Q. for amn. 15th to am.		
	12.9.17		Testing Set. 122, 123, 124 SB Group. Ann. 10841 Answer 1320	Test	Q.R
			made Rotation		
	13.9.17		Testing Set. 122, 123, 124 SB Group. Ann. 10993 Answer 1311	Norr	Q.R
			None Stratin		

WAR DIARY
INTELLIGENCE SUMMARY
(Erase heading not required.)

Army Form C. 2118.

Place	Date	Hour	Summary of Events and Information		Remarks and references to Appendices
	14.9.17		INF & RMS Today Str. 122.123.124. 2B. Group - Men 11205 Animals 1304	Dull	QMG
			New Base + B.H.Q. bivys made for personnel. Stables now WATOU CAPPEL 122 + 124 the group refu-		
			at X.12.d.0 an area for 123 Bn Grp, and refu at X.11.d.7. 124 extend Supply dump		
			site coming in les eqp bivys at HAZEBROUCK being used for conception B"		
	15.9.17		Today Str. 122.123 124 2B Group - Men 11165 Animals 1316	Fine	QMG
			Move to ZEVECOTEN.		
	16.9.17	8.35 a.m. 3.5	Today Str. 122.123 124 3B Group - Men 11175 Animals 1317	Fine	QMG
			Railhead change to OUDERDOM. Supplies now taken direct by B Ech A/C & Coy from Railhead with ??		
			Supplies on leaving Railhead are examined & confirmed correct.		
	17.9.17		Today Str. Men 12014 Animals 2077	Fine	QMG
			140 Bde A"Base from Sub Park. Rain again at 189 Bde R.F.C. Transit		
	18.9.17		Today Str. Men 14571 Animals 3065.	Dull	QMG
			Issue of Clothing item of Signets of the expands at Sext kept. Also Div. Troops at present exhibit & 3.9 PM		
			will come on to HQ Div Park for 21st instant.		
	19.9.17		Today Str : Men 14890 Animals 3092. U.19th return for conception 19th + 20th were delivered.	Fine	QMG
			For 122 124 Lyd Brs 123.98 + 41st D.T's ?? made.		

WAR DIARY or INTELLIGENCE SUMMARY

Army Form C. 2118.

(Erase heading not required.)

Place	Date	Hour	Summary of Events and Information	Remarks and references to Appendices
J.35.c.3.5.	20.9.17		Feeding str. Men 15252 Animals 3107	
			Horse Routine	Weather Showery
				Q.R
	21.9.17		Feeding str. Men 20182 Animals 5292	
			An copy of the Div Operation Order by A.A.Q 39 Div sent for Div Super Staff & Retained	
			Moved Div Headquarters	Fine Q.R
	22.9.17		Feeding str. Men 20061 Animals 5291	
			Tx relieve 2 Bde of R Bde (fm 3rd M3 R.Bde) for arrangement 23rd & previous	Dull Q.R
	23.9.17		Feeding str. Men 15339 Animals 5340	
			41st Div (less artillery) move to CAESTRE. 3 Infantry Bdes detrain by Long fm OUDERDOM and they in new area	
			39.1.9 detail by M.3 to assist transport & animals D.A 40th to feed by 39th Div Div. Railhead at	
			39.19 Amuseries 15 wire F6 to H.Qny K.12.d.0. 39 Div	Fine Q.R
CAESTRE			COMBAT of CAESTRE Steads and full cards Hays Oats & Johns Ete 15 K.12.d.0. 39 Div	
	24.9.17		Feeding str. Men 10918 Animals 1619 Draws by H.T. for Brigade	
			Usual Routine	Fine Q.R
	25.9.17		Feeding str. Men 12474 Animals 1766 228, 233, 237 Fd. Coy + 19 Middlesex Work	
			for ground area and for former Supply Dispatch and broke by rain Transport 26th + 27th in this area of 49 2nd Echo Battalion come in Railhead for Div	Fine
			Div. Ammunition 15 wire 15 4 Army (XV Corp). 123 Bde Transport moved this day by road	Q.R

A6943 Wt. W11422/M1160 350,000 12/16 D. D. & L. Forms/C/2118/14.

WAR DIARY
INTELLIGENCE SUMMARY

Army Form C. 2118.

Place	Date	Hour	Summary of Events and Information		Remarks and references to Appendices
CAESTRE	26.9.17		Fieldry A.T. 122, 123, 124 9 Bon. Men 12801 Anual 1708	Draft	Q.F.
		10730	game on Railhead for Rn Rn		
			123 93. Ringon issued this day.		
LA PANNE	27.9.17		Fieldry Bn: 122, 123, 124 9 Bon. Men 12487 Animals 1780. 123 93. arms 28" and all by tay.	True	Q.F.
			124 93. Ringon issued this day. Rations for 123 93. arms 28" and all by tay.		
	28.9.17		Fieldry A.T. 122, 123, 124 9 Bon. Men 14205 Animals 3286	True	Q.F.
			122 + 123 J.B. draw for OOSTHOEK by tay. Rations for 124 93. and all for CAESTRE by tay.		
			2nd 14th A.H.A. Bde + 25th A.F.A. Bde for reception 30th + movies (124 93)		
	29.9.17		Fieldry A.T. 122, 123, 124 9 Bon. Men 14179 Animals 3457	True	Q.F.
			122 + 123 93. draw for OOSTHOEK by horse transport - 124 93. by tay. Rations + remounts the		
			three groups with all issued by H.T.		
			X Bn's am R 27st that 41 Div. Coys will be attached to 21st Ord. for 30 inst.		
	30.9.17		Fieldry A.T. 122, 123, 124 9 Bon. Men 14345 Animals 3443	True	Q.F.
			100Y. Men 268 Aspit 617		
			Windle 4th Army R.O. (S.S.4.7.)		

Signed
A.D.O. 41st Division
Major

Army Form C. 2118.

WAR DIARY
INTELLIGENCE SUMMARY
(Erase heading not required.)

Instructions regarding War Diaries and Intelligence Summaries are contained in F. S. Regs., Part II. and the Staff Manual respectively. Title pages will be prepared in manuscript.

Place	Date	Hour	Summary of Events and Information	Weather	Remarks and references to Appendices
LA PANNE	1.10.17		Feeding 122 : 123 : 124 Bde – Men 14,135 Rations 3409	Fine	Q.P
			238 M.G.Coy. Our round with first two days rations last night therefore a heavy draw. Summary		
			Strength that 650 too few for purposes of rations for remainder Oct 1,2,3,-7		
	2.10.17		Feeding Div : 122 : 123 : 127 Bde - Men 16,831 Rations 3399	Fine	Q.P
			4500 R. Rations drawn for R.A.O.		
			1st 4th Brigade 15th 6, 7, 8, 9 at LEFFRINCKOUCKE Bn 1st 5 fit 6 (13th coy Q – Q.S. 7 30.9.17)		
			had rations from 15th coy Q. – 14th A.H.A.B.		
	3.10.17		Feeding Div 122 : 123 : 127 Bde – Men 15,856 Rations 1379	Dull	Q.P
			Roads Rotten. "Fog, mystic of landing activities on Railhead"		
	4.10.17		Feeding Div : 122 : 123 : 124 Bde – Men 14,247 Rations 2462	Dull + Wet	P.P
			Receiving of Forage Hmi + Brab – 43% + 72% respectively		
	5.10.17		Feeding Div : 122 : 123 : 124 Bde – Men 13,732 Rations 2420	Wet and cold	Q.P
			123rd Bde now 15 forward area		
	6.10.17		Feeding Div : 122 : 123 : 124 Bde – Men 12,694 Rations 2426	Wet	Q.P
			124th Bde now 15 forward area		
ST IDESBALDE	7.10.17		Feeding Div : 122 : 123 : 124 IDesbe 32nd DivDispersed	fine	Q.P
			Railhead Change at ST IDESBALDE June one first day from A.S.O. 42 Div stuck no supplies of fresh		
			H.A.S.D. 32 Div. later out my rations stuck. Stuck from Railhead in light Railway.		

Wt. W11422/M1160 350,000 12/16 D. D. & L. Forms/C/2118/14.
A6945

Army Form C. 2118.

WAR DIARY
INTELLIGENCE SUMMARY
(Erase heading not required.)

Place	Date	Hour	Summary of Events and Information	Weather	Remarks and references to Appendices
SEC. IDESBALDE	8.10.17		Feeding Str: 122, 123, 124, J.Odr: 32nd Div Corps Men 18252. Animals 5833. Percentage of Frozen Meat & Bread - 62% & 77% respectively. Authority received from 15" Corps Q. to issue Rum daily if required	Gale	GR
	9.10.17		Feeding Str: 122, 123, 124, J.Odr: 32nd Div Corps Men 19311. Animals 5914. Usual Routine. Delay in of issuing frozen due to light Rly mistake	Hvy Lightning	GR
	10.10.17		Feeding Str: 122, 123, 134, J.Odr: 32nd Div Corps Men 18966. Animals 5883. Percentage of Frozen Meat & Bread - 61% & 72% respectively. Supplies arranged from Railhead to Refilling point by M.T. owing to light Rly not being available.	Windy	GR
	11.10.17		Feeding Str: 122, 123, 134, J.Odr: 32nd Div Corps Men 18934. Animals 5885. Usual Routine. Percentage Frozen Meat & Bread 59% & 72% respectively. 78 Tons Coal received from 15" IDESBALDE Railhead	Fine	GR
	12.10.17		Feeding Str: 122, 123, 124, J.Odr: 32nd Div Corps Men 19815. Animals 6591. Usual Routine. Percentage Frozen Meat & Bread 60% & 79% respectively. Under instructions from 41st Div.Q. 139 Fd Ambulance to be returned by O.R. Rc. for consumption 16" inst. and onwards	Dull	GR
				Wet	GR

WAR DIARY or INTELLIGENCE SUMMARY

Army Form C. 2118.

(Erase heading not required.)

Instructions regarding War Diaries and Intelligence Summaries are contained in F.S. Regs., Part II, and the Staff Manual respectively. Title pages will be prepared in manuscript.

Place	Date	Hour	Summary of Events and Information	Weather	Remarks and references to Appendices
ST ISSBALDE	12.10.17		Feeding Str. 123rd, 133rd & 134th J. Btns + Men 20229. Animals 7563. 32nd Div. Troops. Usual routine. Percentage Bread & Meat 73% & 58% respectively.	Showery	GR
	14.10.17		Feeding Strength Div. Troops 122nd, 123rd, 124th J. Btns – Men 19062. Animals 7432. 32nd Div. Troops.	Fine	GR
		10.00	Iron Rations drawn for some 15 inst. Owing to light Rly. not being available at usual time considerable delay was caused in off loading for train.		
	15.10.17		Div. Troops arrive in forward area. Feeding Str. 122nd, 123rd, 124th Inf. Btn Div. Troops & 32nd Div. Troops. Men 19199. Animals 8090. Early loading on light Rly commenced. Usual routine.	Fine	GR
	16.10.17		Feeding St. Div. Troops 123rd, 124th Inf. Btn, 32nd Div. Troops – Men 21139. Animals 8089. 4000 Iron Rations trucks despatched received from Puchevoc Guard 10.17.	Fine	GR
			32nd Div. Troops draw for the last time from our Rest train. Percentage of Bread & Meat 69% & 65% respectively.		
	17.10.17		Feeding Str. Div. Troops 123rd, 124th F.B. 123rd, 124th J. Otes – Men 17853. Animals 5765. Percentage of Bread & Meat 78% & 62% respectively. Usual routine. Fine. United Army Headquarters (cafe, coffee)		GR

WAR DIARY

INTELLIGENCE SUMMARY

(Erase heading not required.)

Army Form C. 2118.

Place	Date	Hour	Summary of Events and Information	Weather	Remarks and references to Appendices
ST ADELBALDE	18/10/17		Feeding Str - Ord' Troops 122"' 123"' & 124" I/Rdn - Men 18127. Animals 5781. Usual routine Percentage Bread & Meat 76% & 60% respectively	Fine	Q.R
	19/10/17		Feeding Str - Ord' Troops. 122"' 122"' & 124" I/Rdn - Men 17839. Animals 5062. 39" Ldv R.F.A. move to SYNTHE area night of 18" inst. rations for tomorrow when 30" inst not carried to new area by M.T. 19" inst. Brigade draw from this Division for its last time	Fine	Q.R
	20/10/17		Feeding Str - Ord' Troops 122"' 123"' 124" I/Rdn - Men 17807. Animals 5061. Usual routine Percentage Bread & Meat 78% & 62% respectively	Fine	R.Q
	21/10/17		Feeding Str - Ord' Troops. 122"' 123"' 124" I/Rdn - Men 17442. Animals 5055. Usual routine Percentage Bread & Meat 79% & 63% respectively	Fine	Q.R
	22/10/17		Feeding Str - Ord' Troops. 122"' 123"' 124" I/Rdn - Men 17408. Animals 5044. Usual routine Percentage Bread & Meat 75% & 58% respectively	Fine	Q.R
	23.10.17		Feeding Str: of persons - Men 16874 Animals 4945	Wet	Q.R
	24.10.17		Feeding Str - Men 16705 Animals 4934 & Ind 158 A.F.A. Bde til last Fri 23" midnight Rail ration required til 27" & 28" inst.		Q.R
	25.10.17		Feeding Str - Men 16327 Animals 5015 Usual Routine.	Fine	Q.R

Army Form C. 2118.

WAR DIARY
INTELLIGENCE SUMMARY
(Erase heading not required.)

Instructions regarding War Diaries and Intelligence Summaries are contained in F. S. Regs., Part II. and the Staff Manual respectively. Title pages will be prepared in manuscript.

Place	Date	Hour	Summary of Events and Information	Remarks and references to Appendices
ST IDESBALDE	26.10.17		Fighting Str. Ren. H1886. Arrivals 4895	Jan.
			Arty. Group at Brillard 13 Hrs of H.D. horse	
	27.10.17		Fighting Str. Ren. 15307. Arrivals 4967. Foger Huis 59 R Brig 79 R S.G. Brit. Veg	Jan.
			Horse Rations	
	28.10.17		Fighting str. Ren. 16007. Arrivals 5062.	Jan.
			127 JB from KETEGHEM area.	
	29.10.17		Fighting Str. Ren. 16355. Arrivals 5044. B.H.Q. move to Rue de Luges. T.H.Q. to 40 Rue de Luges.	Attach w/ attached loads fwd to 15 A.D.O. G. & Sw
			ROSENDAEL. 124 JB. take over 9th Div. Rn. in our area of corp. 30th. Relief of 9th Div. taken over 127 JB.	
40 Rue de Luges			Arty of 9th Div at ST IDESBALDE. 124 JB. arrs for LEEFRINKOUCKE — Arty. group from ST IDESBALDE	
Rosendael	30.10.17		Fighting Str. Ren. 15857. Arrivals 3926. 122 JB. & 127 JB. arrs for LEEFRINKOUCKE — other	Jan.
			Group ST IDESBALDE.	
	31.10.17		Fighting Str. Ren. 17463. Arrivals 4371. Relieved for state Divison. changes to LEEFRINKOUCKE	Jan.

Army Form C. 2118.

WAR DIARY
INTELLIGENCE SUMMARY.
(Erase heading not required.)

Place	Date	Hour	Summary of Events and Information	Remarks and references to Appendices
CAMPOSAMPIERO	1.3.18		41st Division commence to entrain for FRANCE. First train on to contain portion of 1 Bay going to train journey, four and three personnel returning to be picked up on the way	Finis. Q.R.
CAMPOSAMPIERO	2.3.18		A.Q. H'dts train cleared down offers and entrain	Finis Q.R.
	3.4.3.18		train journey	Finis. Q.R.
LUCHEUX	5.3.18		Arrive [?] at DOULLENS, detrain and move to LUCHEUX where train offrs & gunrs all kit decanning, later with the remainder portion of train which follows to rear day's journey received rations in [?] major. Horses picketed for the present	Finis. Q.R.
LUCHEUX	6.3.18		Horses continue to arrive.	Finis Q.R.
LUCHEUX	7.3.18		[?] to track train being atched too run acrosstopish S.S. & I. 3rd Bay to relieve relief of trucks & ft. [?] daily allotment. = Theresa portion of Div. Arty not [?] [?] arrd. trains.	Finis Q.R.
LUCHEUX	8.3.18		Drew for Railhead. Sren Rn. 3536 Annexe Rn. 571- offrs. bat. of horses & ft. met to train	Finis. Q.R.
LUCHEUX	9.3.18		Drew for Railhead. Sren Rn. 10574 Annexe Rn. 1297. Road Routine	Finis. Q.R.
LUCHEUX	10.3.18		Drew for Railhead. Sren Rn. 14235 Annexe Rn. 1851	Finis Q.R.
LUCHEUX	11.3.18		Drew for Railhead. Sren Rn. 14602 Annexe Rn. 1877. Road Routine	Finis Q.R.
LUCHEUX	12.3.18		Drew for Railhead - Sren Rn. 14565 Annexe Rn. 1830. Road Routine	Finis Q.R.
LUCHEUX	13.3.18		Drew for Railway - Sren Rn. 14501 Annexe Rn. 1812. Div. Coy. Provisions all stn. arrived. Main certain quantity of ft. gun, Bound & Vey for Rn in up of S.S. - took [?] advanced personnel.	Finis. Q.R.
LUCHEUX	14.3.18		Drew from Railway - Shew Rn. 16012 Annexe Rn. 3382. Road Routine 1st D.A.C. - there [?] one Army withdrawn formed.	Wet. Q.R.

Army Form C. 2118.

WAR DIARY
INTELLIGENCE SUMMARY.
(Erase heading not required.)

Instructions regarding War Diaries and Intelligence Summaries are contained in F. S. Regs., Part II. and the Staff Manual respectively. Title pages will be prepared in manuscript.

Place	Date	Hour	Summary of Events and Information	Remarks and references to Appendices
LUCHEUX	15.3.19		Drawn for Railhead – Thero Rm 18900 Annals Rm 3339. Horse Ration.	Water Fire
LUCHEUX	16.3.19		Drawn for Railhead – Thero Rm 15127 Annals Rm 2598. Horse Ration.	Fire
LUCHEUX	17.3.19		Drawn for Railhead. Thero Rm 13801 Annals Rm 3910. Horse Ration.	Fire
LUCHEUX	18.3.19		Drawn for Railhead. Thero Rm 15727 Annals Rm 4046. Major P.S. Pritchett proceeded on leave to Havre. Acts for him. Visits were paid to the tongue cap mostly ammo dump some forty emps. and DSW train for the Q branch with D.D.D.J.G. B.S.D.DJG. R.S. and 19th Division forts Blast were examined. 20 ms of issue of ammo to our stroke stuff. Move to XIII Corps area.	Fire
LUCHEUX	19.3.19		Drawn for Rlhd – Thero Rm 1472 Annals Rm 3729. Horse Ration.	Forage Fire
LUCHEUX	20.3.19		Drawn for Rlhd – Thero Rm 4050. Annals Rm 3722. Av. convoy of one for BAIZIEUX – certain transport goes to Dep Horses + Sumas stomach Ration stock. It all takes to convoy for 21st and lefts ST Souplet (one Division) depth and 62 with Ration for one 2nd rest.	Fire
BRESLE	21.3.19		Train Headquarters and 1st BRESLE RP.0: – 122 J.S. RIBEMONT. 123 J.S. BOUZINCOURT. 124 J.S. LAVIEVILLE. Ration drawn for Railhead. Thero Rm 13855 Annals Rm 3712.	Bell Fire
ACHIET-LE-PETIT	22.3.19		Train Headquarters and 1st to ACHIET LE PETIT. Railhead ALBERT. Ration drawn for Railhead. Thero 5340 Annals 3636. Rendezvous due 1st to 4th corps. Taining forward for Train. 22nd inter arrived at 21.00 mr.	Fire
ACHIET LE PETIT	23.3.19		Railhed MIRAUMONT Rm drawn – Thero 19804 Annals 7373. Convoy to five 236. R.A. Bde.	Bee Fire
ACHIET LE PETIT	24.3.19		Railhed MIRAUMONT T.H.Q and 1st BUCQUOY Rm drawn Thero 19825 Annals 7962.	Fire
BIENVILLERS AU BOIS	25.3.19		Railhed COLINCAMPS. T.H.Q moved to ST AMAND. Rm drawn Thero 13040 Annals 7960.	Fire
BAILLEULVAL	26.3.19		Railhed BELLE EGLISE. T.H.Q moved to BAILLEULVAL. Rm drawn Thero 16412 Annals 8293.	Fire
BAILLEULVAL	27.3.19		Railhed – AUTHEULE. Rm drawn Thero 16211 Annals 8489.	Fire

Army Form C. 2118.

WAR DIARY
of
INTELLIGENCE SUMMARY
(Erase heading not required.)

Instructions regarding War Diaries and Intelligence Summaries are contained in F.S. Regs., Part II. and the Staff Manual respectively. Title pages will be prepared in manuscript.

Place	Date	Hour	Summary of Events and Information	Remarks and references to Appendices
GOMBREMETZ.	28.3.18		Move to Main Magasin. Railhead AUTHIEULE. Run draw Ins 8731 Animals 2047	Att. Dec.
AUTHIE.	29.3.18		From to AUTHIE. Railhead AUTHIEULE. Run drawn Ins 9971. Animals 2060	Att. Dec.
AUTHIE	30.3.18		Railhead AUTHIEULE. Run draw Ins 10113 Animals 2000. Drew 3700 Iron Rations from R.S.O. and 500 Iron Rations from 42nd Div. Train to make up deficiency.	Att. Dec.
AUTHIE	31.3.18		Railhead AUTHIEULE. Run drawn Ins 9800 Animals 1958. House Rations.	Att. Dec. Dec.

S.S.O. 41st DIVISION.

Army Form C. 2118.

WAR DIARY
or
INTELLIGENCE SUMMARY.
(Erase heading not required.)

Instructions regarding War Diaries and Intelligence Summaries are contained in F.S. Regs., Part II. and the Staff Manual respectively. Title pages will be prepared in manuscript.

Place	Date	Hour	Summary of Events and Information	Remarks and references to Appendices
1.4.18. AUTHIE			Railhead AUTHIEULE. Rations drawn for Railhead. Inn. 9924. Animals 1537	Nov. AN
	2.4.18		Railhead AUTHIEULE. Rations drawn for Railhead. Inn. 9922. Animals 1629. T.H.Q. moved to HALLOY	Nov. AN
HALLOY				
STEENVOORDE	3.4.18		Railhead SAULTY. Rations drawn for Railhead. Inn. 9757. Animals 1835. Issues to army from there by second lin. Coys — T.H.Q. moved to STEENVOORDE	Dec. AN
STEENVOORDE	4.4.18		Railhead change to WIPPENHOEK. Rations drawn for Railhead. Inn. 9374. Animals 1824. Division entrained on 3rd and 4th from PREVENT & PT. HOUVIN [illegible] 3rd and [illegible] trains [illegible] with rations for 123 [illegible] for [illegible] Div. transfer [illegible] 124 [illegible] hay rations for the [illegible]	Dec. AN
STEENVOORDE	5.4.18		Railhead drawn Inn. 9389 Animals 1830 – Also 2052 extra rations drawn for recuperating [illegible]	Dec. AN
STEENVOORDE	6.4.18		Rations drawn for Railhead – Inn. 14140. Animals 1839. Also 2899 extra rations drawn for recuperating [illegible]	Dec. CoSM
STEENVOORDE	7.4.18		Rations drawn for Railhead – Inn. 13696. Animals 1638. Horse Rations.	Dec. CoSM
STEENVOORDE	8.4.18		Rations drawn for Railhead – Inn. 14367. Animals 1842.	Dec. CoSM
STEENVOORDE	9.4.18		One day flee Ammn sent [illegible] to Armd as M.T. 65 — 123 V3, en CAESTRE 122 + 124 V3 en VLAMERTINGE. Took in fuel dump of 69th Div at VLAMERTINGE.	Dec. CoSM
Also ST. Cm.30	10.4.18		Move to stage camp Issued 13 system lorries to H.T. for VLAMERTINGE Railhead. Drew rations for this Railhead and by 29th Div 49th Div. Corps drew from our fuel [illegible] feeding [illegible] Inn. 15677 Animals 19.12	Dec. CoSM
"	11.4.18		Railhead change to PROVEN – drew to M.T. Rations Inn. 21341 Animals 4832	Inn. CoSM
"	12.4.18		Railhead still PROVEN. Rations drawn Men. 22136 Animals 4693.	Inn. CoSM

WAR DIARY

INTELLIGENCE SUMMARY

(Erase heading not required.)

Army Form C. 2118.

Instructions regarding War Diaries and Intelligence Summaries are contained in F. S. Regs., Part II. and the Staff Manual respectively. Title pages will be prepared in manuscript.

Place	Date	Hour	Summary of Events and Information	Hour	Remarks and references to Appendices
About 28 G.4.a.3.0	13.4.18		Railhead PROVEN - Rations drawn from 22172. Amounts 4990. A.L.D 59 Div. Loads on return trip to be passed on to Dump nearer to or	Fine	WSM
do.	14.4.18		Rear train late at PROVEN. Rations drawn from 15352. Amounts 3867. Lois feeding ests due to inadequate lighting of 29th D.S.	Bett getting.	WSM
do.	15.4.18		Rear train again late at PROVEN. Rations drawn from 17199. Amounts 3871	Sun getting.	WSM
do.	16.4.18		Railhead PROVEN. Rations drawn from 16858. Amounts 3853	Dull	WSM
do.	17.4.18		Railhead PESELHOEK - but owing to shelling, Train was moved to PROVEN where supplies were issued. Rations drawn from 17167. Amounts 3845.	Wet	WSM
do.	18.4.18		Draw from PROVEN by H.T. Rations drawn from 17396. Amounts 3839	Wet. Misty	WSM
do.	19.4.18		Draw from PROVEN by M.T. Rations drawn from 17374. Amounts 3854	Fair	WSM
do.	20.4.18		Draw from PROVEN by M.T. Rations drawn from 17157. Amounts 3832	Fair	WSM
do.	21.4.18		Draw from PROVEN by M.T. Rations drawn from 17794. Amounts 3528. Shops P.N. reported returned for leave plant evening, and recover duties as Senior Supply Officer.	Fine	WSM
do.	22.4.18		Draw from PROVEN by M.T. Rations drawn from 17339. Amounts 3851	Fine	PMP
do.	23.4.18		Draw from PROVEN by M.T. Rations drawn from 17717. Amounts 3853	Fine	PMP
do.	24.4.18		Railhead PROVEN - by M.T. Rations drawn from 16995. Amounts 3859	Dull	PMP
do.	25.4.18		Railhead PROVEN - by M.T. Rations drawn from 17548. Amounts 3844	Fine	PMP
do.	26.4.18		Railhead PROVEN - by M.T. Rations drawn from 17551. Amounts 3869. Move to PESELHOEK.	do.	PMP
do.	27.4.18		Railhead PROVEN by M.T. Rations drawn from 17405. Amounts 36.78	do.	PMP

PROVEN - PEPERINGHE Road

WAR DIARY
INTELLIGENCE SUMMARY
(Erase heading not required.)

Army Form C. 2118.

Place	Date	Hour	Summary of Events and Information	Remarks and references to Appendices
Sheet 27 F.21 d.3.2	28.4.18		Drew from PROVEN by H.T. Rations drawn Sec. 17647. Remounts 3998. Forward to rail-head to issue rations to 1/1 Yorkshire Dragoons below Bn.	O/C Q
"	29.4.18		Was to delay at PROVEN from train taken to ROUSBRUGGE - drew by M.T. Rations drew Sec. 17285. Remounts 4045. Supply train from my unit.	O/C Q
	30.4.18		Drew from Rec. Dump at H.M.T. by Sec. 13990. Remounts 1863 (for 3 Rec. Group of 41st Div.) & H.T. Sec. Refill (and sent cart to pick. D (by road of 41 Div. 2) Drew for Recon issued on ST OMER by M.T. Sec. 17163. Remounts 3915. Rations drawn and delivered to enemy. No problem to remark.	O/C Q

Army Form C. 2118.

WAR DIARY
INTELLIGENCE SUMMARY.
(Erase heading not required.)

Instructions regarding War Diaries and Intelligence Summaries are contained in F. S. Regs., Part II. and the Staff Manual respectively. Title pages will be prepared in manuscript.

Place	Date	Hour	Summary of Events and Information	Weather	Remarks and references to Appendices
March 27 Feb 1/2	1.5.18		Draw fm ST. OMER by M.T. Ration draw fm 16863 Animals 3941	Dull	QMS
do	2.5.18		Draw fm ST. OMER by M.T. Ration draw fm 17261 Animals 3943	Fine	QMS
do	3.5.18		Draw fm ROUSBRUGGE Railhead by M.T. Ration draw Men 17135 Animals 3926	Fine	QMS
do	4.5.18		Draw fm ROUSBRUGGE by M.T. Ration draw Men 17071 Animals 3930	Fine	QMS
do	5.5.18		Draw fm ROUSBRUGGE by M.T. Ration draw Men 17171 Animals 3868	Dull	QMS
do	6.5.18		Railhead - ROUSBRUGGE - 10th and onwards draw fm supply by M.T. to arrive 10 lorries convoy fully load at 9.0 AM. Ration draw Men 16729 Animals 3865	Fair	QMS
do	7.5.18		Railhead - ROUSBRUGGE. Ration draw Men 16854 Animals 3876	Fair	QMS
do	8.5.18		Railhead - ROUSBRUGGE - Ration train fm 16907 Animals 3881. drawn was of fine weather out today on sky.	Fine	QMS
do	9.5.18		Railhead - ROUSBRUGGE. Ration draw Men 16957 Animals 3882	Fine	QMS
do	10.5.18		Railhead - ROUSBRUGGE. Ration draw Men 16835 Animals 3881	Dull	QMS
do	11.5.18		Railhead - ROUSBRUGGE. Ration draw Men 16909 Animals 3869. Fmn 781 Area Employ Coy (div) 70 13.4.18	Dull	QMS
do	12.5.18		Railhead - ROUSBRUGGE. Ration draw Men 16858 Animals 3858	Rain	QMS
do	13.5.18		Railhead - ROUSBRUGGE. Ration draw Men 16730 Animals 3872 (SS37 4/12.5.18) 1500 Jon Ration fm U.S.O. was authd. S.S.A. to Div Army to be taken on Nueva J. 124. J. Bn.	Rain	QMS
do	14.5.18		Railhead - ROUSBRUGGE. Ration draw Men 16634 Animals 3793 (29 D.A. draw fm 156th inn Sce soi 4.6.7 11 Mala Junction for Battern transport 16th nov. to.	Dull	QMS

Army Form C. 2118.

WAR DIARY

INTELLIGENCE SUMMARY.

(Erase heading not required.)

Instructions regarding War Diaries and Intelligence Summaries are contained in F. S. Regs., Part II. and the Staff Manual respectively. Title pages will be prepared in manuscript.

Place	Date	Hour	Summary of Events and Information		Remarks and references to Appendices
LA LOVIE CHATEAU Also 27-Feb'd.29	15.5.18		Move to place marked, 29th D.A. area to last line shots Appx B.R. Area from km for Sec I.S.D. Ration draw from ROUSBRUGGE. The 17762 Animals 5234.	Fine	S/R
do	16.5.15		Ration draw from ROUSBRUGGE - Men 17711 Animals 3916.	Fine	S/R
do	17.5.15		Ration draw from ROUSBRUGGE - Men 17224 Anim 3911. Horse Routine S.D.2.15. Horse cmd.	Fine	S/R
do	18.5.15		Ration draw from ROUSBRUGGE - Men 17334 Anim 3915. The A M.M.G. Batt. attack by the bn. Min A Candn. hosp. 10, 4, 7 & 11 reaction. G.R.19th and M.D.B. retired to 20th inst.	Fine	S/R
do	19.5.15		Ration draw from ROUSBRUGGE - Men 16902 Anim 3860. Horse Routine	Fine	S/R
do	20.5.15		Ration draw from ROUSBRUGGE - Men 17500 Anim 3861	Fine	S/R
do	21.5.15		Ration draw from ROUSBRUGGE - Men 17381 Anim 3570. Horse Routine.	Fine	S/R
do	22.5.15		Ration draw from ROUSBRUGGE - Men 17778 Anim 3870. Horse Routine	Fine	S/R
do	23.5.15		Ration draw from ROUSBRUGGE - Men 17505 Anim 3889. Horse Routine.	Fine	S/R
do	24.5.15		Ration draw from ROUSBRUGGE - Men 17373 Anim 3855. Horse Routine.	Fair	S/R
do	25.5.15		Ration draw from ROUSBRUGGE - Men 17131 Anim 3761. Horse Routine.	Fine	S/R
do	26.5.15		Ration draw from ROUSBRUGGE - Men 17214 Anim 3883. Horse Routine.	Dull	S/R
do	27.5.15		Ration draw from ROUSBRUGGE - Men 17385 Anim 3795. Horse Routine.	Fine	S/R
do	28.5.15		Ration draw from ROUSBRUGGE - Men 17079 Anim 3900. Horse Routine.	Fine	S/R

Army Form C. 2118.

WAR DIARY
or
INTELLIGENCE SUMMARY.
(Erase heading not required.)

Instructions regarding War Diaries and Intelligence Summaries are contained in F. S. Regs., Part II. and the Staff Manual respectively. Title pages will be prepared in manuscript.

Place	Date	Hour	Summary of Events and Information	Weather	Remarks and references to Appendices
LA LOVIE CHATEAU Aux 27 FLOODING	29.5.18		Railhead ROUSBRUGGE – Rations drawn from 17341 Amount 3921	Fine	
	30.5.18		Railhead ROUSBRUGGE – Rations drawn from 17535 Amount 3844	Fine	
	31.5.18		Railhead ROUSBRUGGE – Rations drawn from 17293 Amount 3841. Issue Rations.	Fine	

S.S.O. 41ST DIVISION.

Army Form C. 2118.

WAR DIARY

INTELLIGENCE SUMMARY.
(Erase heading not required.)

Instructions regarding War Diaries and Intelligence Summaries are contained in F.S. Regs., Part II. and the Staff Manual respectively. Title pages will be prepared in manuscript.

Place	Date	Hour	Summary of Events and Information	Weather	Remarks and references to Appendices
LA LOBIE CHATEAU (nr FEBUIN)	1.6.18		Railhead ROUSBRUGGE - Ration drawn from 17114. Annuis 3837	Fine	G.R.
"	2.6.18		Railhead ROUSBRUGGE - Rats drawn from 17073. Annuis 3872. Ration column to turn again to Pack train.	Fine	G.R.
"	3.6.18		Railhead ROUSBRUGGE - Ration drawn from 15153. Annuis 3867. Bn. arranged to be relieved by 49 Div. and proceed to Z. An Survey Coy. Bn. Hy. remain in line for present. An Limbers of 1.3 Sqd Bns. in forward Ry. route taken to unloading of mages in stages via - ZEGGERS CAPPEL - ROUSBRUGGE, the supply train gives also 0. 49 Div. takes over attached Bns. of 1st own Supt. Coy., and also the ration column for first day.	Fine	G.R.
NIEURLET (nr St OMER)	4.6.18		New rail head area. B.H.Q. now at NIEURLET. Railhead ROUSBRUGGE - Jhn. 14808 Annuis 38/5	Fine	G.R.
"	5.6.18		Railhead changed to WATTEN. Ration for 41 D.A. R'ld 5th. 6. 7. 4th arrived 2nd by 4. Rail. Jhn Watten drew Jhn. WATTEN for 3 St. Bn. Groups Jhn. 14823 Annuis 1780 at ROUSBRUGGE Ration drawn from ROUSBRUGGE for R.A. (Jhn. 2315 Annuis 2028)	Fine	G.R.
"	6.6.18		Ration drawn from WATTEN for 3 St Bde Groups. Jhn. 12923 Annuis 1511 ROUSBRUGGE for D.A. Jhn 2337 Annuis 20.23.	Fine	G.R.
EPERLECQUES	7.6.18		Bde (with B.N.Q.) 45 place approached road ration drawn for WATTEN Jhn. 12884 Annuis 1810 Ration draw for ROUSBRUGGE for D.A. Jhn 2311 Annuis 20.45.	Fine	G.R.
"	8.6.18		41st D.A. moved to POLINCOVE Area Railhead for D.A. 6th 7th 10th BLENDECQUES Ration drawn from Jhn 2328 Annuis 2030 (h.M.T.) 3 Rifles drew by H.T. from WATTEN Jhn 14381 Annuis 1732. 1.3. armd. mtd. to BONNINGUES area.	Fine	G.R.
"	9.6.18		124 J.B. to Bdy. & ration draws by M.T. on 122 & 123 JB by H.T. for WATTEN Ration draw by Jhn 14331 Annuis Bett of 1 Bn Group going for 3 Rifle Group established fact taken fr rail drawing 1322. Railhead nr Arnele Ration drawn from WATTEN Jhn 2294 Annuis 2149.	Fine	G.R.
"	10.6.18		123 J.B. Hqrs. St MARTIN AU LAERT Area. Draw nr by M.T. Ration draw fr WATTEN 13615 Ration draws from BLENDECQUES for D.A. - Jhn. 2448 Annuis 2227	Fine	G.R.

WAR DIARY

INTELLIGENCE SUMMARY

(Erase heading not required.)

Army Form C. 2118.

Instructions regarding War Diaries and Intelligence Summaries are contained in F.S. Regs., Part II. and the Staff Manual respectively. Title pages will be prepared in manuscript.

Place	Date	Hour	Summary of Events and Information		Remarks and references to Appendices
ETERLECQUES	11.6.19		Returns to D.A. showing HATTEN the drawer for Div. – Jun. 15833 Animals 3943. The day before for 310 Artillery and Supply Column – they draft below are not here employed: any second ration for whole Division. B.I.D. are now about by H.T.	Fine	QR
	12.6.19		Ration drawn from WATTEN – Men 15861 Animals 3800. Rather Restive.	Fine	QR
	13.6.19		Ration drawn from WATTEN – Men 15793 Animals 3963	Fine	QR
	14.6.19		Ration drawn for WATTEN – Men 15653 Animals 3909.	Dull	QR
	15.6.19		Ration Hot Ors king fit in am. 16 x.a. Ration drawn for WATTEN – Men 16513 Animals 3842.	Fine	QR
	16.6.19		Ration drawn from WATTEN – Men 16640 Animals 3883. Horses to go to ARQUES for Shoeing. Left the forge	Fine	QR
	17.6.19		Ration drawn for WATTEN – Men 16905 Animals 3887. Rains Rations	Dull	QR
	18.6.19		Ration drawn from WATTEN – Men 18291 Animals 3882. Draw two days ration for See Rangliss. troop, so that they have their second days ration instead of them being drawn sub below.	Fine	QR
	19.6.19		Ration drawn for WATTEN – Men 17560 Animals 3874. Both second H.T. horses at Vanilla. That group sends very small convoy	Rain	QR
	20.6.19		Ration drawn for WATTEN – Men 16805 Animals 3870.	Fine	QR
	21.6.19		Ration drawn for WATTEN – Men 16575 Animals 3869. Rains Rations.	Fair	QR
	22.6.19		Ration drawn for WATTEN – Men 16927 Animals 3867. Rains Rations. Parade DBSJ 2.45am.	Rain	QR
	23.6.19		Ration drawn for WATTEN – Men 16840 Animals 3892. Rains Rations.	Dull	QR
	24.6.19		Ration drawn for WATTEN – Men 16807 Animals 3841. Rains Rations.	Rain	QR
	25.6.19		Ration drawn for WATTEN – Men 16782 Animals 3859. Find Sen. Reception kept ft last line Division more practical – hunting for engine in string down. (by M.T.)	Fine	QR

Army Form C. 2118.

WAR DIARY
INTELLIGENCE SUMMARY.
(Erase heading not required.)

Instructions regarding War Diaries and Intelligence Summaries are contained in F.S. Regs., Part II. and the Staff Manual respectively. Title pages will be prepared in manuscript.

Place	Date	Hour	Summary of Events and Information	Remarks and references to Appendices
CODEZEELE.	21.6.18		Rations drawn from WATTEN Jun 15030. Report 3872. All ground open by M.T. S.W.Q. now to offices requiring same. Ration dumps in rest area in fact use.	
	23.6.18		Rations drawn from WATTEN. Rec. 14884. Account 3743. Horse Ration.	
	25.6.18		Rations drawn from WATTEN. Rec. 14656. Account 3844. Horse Ration.	
	29.6.18		Railway change to ESQUELBECQ – supplies sent from there by motor lorry arrive to STEENVOORDE by T dump. Rations 36 for lifted by mules (by M.T.) Rations arrive Rec. 14629. Account 3903. Horse Rations arrived from ESQUELBECQ. Rec. 6344.	
	30.6.18		M.T. lorries of Reserve Park and details to HQ to compensate for shortage at ration dump (and Self supply ration days had been sent off) line to actual supply line to STEENVOORDE. Thus a train 8am – 10am Degrees Rich 16255 Account 3902. Till Rec. 12744 Account 3915. Rations drawn from R.Pk.	

MAJOR.

Army Form C. 2118.

WAR DIARY
INTELLIGENCE SUMMARY.
(Erase heading not required.)

Instructions regarding War Diaries and Intelligence Summaries are contained in F. S. Regs., Part II. and the Staff Manual respectively. Title pages will be prepared in manuscript.

Place	Date	Hour	Summary of Events and Information		Remarks and references to Appendices
OUDEZEELE	1.7.18		Ration drawn – Men 14509 Animals 3881. Naval Routine.	Fine	A.R.
Shed 27 K21 b 8 35.	2.7.18		Ration drawn – Men 14405 Animals 3865. Move to camp anyway near.	Fine	A.R.
"	3.7.18		Ration drawn – Men 14776 Animals 3867. Naval Routine	Dull	A.R.
	4.7.18		Ration drawn for Railhead – Men 14267 Animals 3868. Naval Routine	Fine	A.R.
	5.7.18		Ration drawn for Railhead – Men 14949 Animals 3827. Bonous & feed 5th Baton by K.E.F. for cav. 6th & goats	Dull	A.R.
	6.7.18		Ration drawn for Railhead – Men 15077 Animals 3831. Naval Routine	Fine	A.R.
	7.7.18		Ration drawn for Railhead. Men 14619 Animals 3834 Naval Routine	Fine	A.R.
	8.7.18		Ration drawn for Railhead – Men 14726 Animals 3863. Naval Routine	Dull	A.R.
	9.7.18		Ration drawn for Railhead. Men 15983 Animals 4737. These figures include 150 A.F.A. Bde which is to be retained by this Divn. for reception 10th Cavalry.	Fine	A.R.
	10.7.18		Ration drawn for Railhead & for 16011 Animals 4714. Naval Routine Men 14243 of ration drawn went being "trains" in (i.e. no no horses) trains 12th & 13th inst.) (Unknown maintenance for roads & refits trains made as Up.	Rain	A.R.
	11.7.18		Ration drawn for Railhead Mem 16578 Animals 4735. Naval Routine	Wet	A.R.
	12.7.18		Ration drawn for Railhead Men 16263 Animals 4781 Naval Routine.	Fine	A.R.
	13.7.18		Ration drawn for Railhead Men 17143 Animals 5609 This includes hay for main forage for 150" A.F.A. Bde. hay for this field on to the mail freight on the Rhine	Dull	A.R.
	14.7.18		Ration drawn for Railhead – Men 16059 Animals 4650 Naval Routine	Rain	A.R.
	15.7.18		Ration drawn for Railhead – Men 16142 Animals 4597 Naval Routine	Rain	A.R.

WAR DIARY

INTELLIGENCE SUMMARY

Army Form C. 2118.

Place	Date	Hour	Summary of Events and Information		Remarks and references to Appendices
Sheet 27 K 21 b 8 5	16.7.15		Rations drawn for R'Hd. Sheet 16049 Amount 4701. Normal Routine.	Supply	QMS
	17.7.15		Rations drawn for R'Hd. Sheet 17376 (reduce 2nd day for nonpayment) Amount 4690	Sup	QMS
	18.7.15		Rations drawn for R'Hd. Sheet 16371 Amount 4690. Normal Routine.	Fin	QMS
	19.7.15		Rations drawn for R'Hd. Sheet 16559 Amount 4697. Normal Routine.	Fin	QMS
	20.7.15		Rations drawn for R'Hd. Sheet 16491 Amount 4697. Normal Routine.	Wed	QMS
	21.7.15		Rations drawn for R'Hd. Sheet 10103 Amount 4640. No ration returned by no 4. Fren.	Fren	QMS
	22.7.15		Rations drawn for Railhead Sheet 16061 Amount 4648. Normal Routine.	Sat	QMS
	23.7.15		Rations drawn for Railhead Sheet 15937 Amount 4642. Normal Routine.		QMS
	24.7.15		Rations drawn for Railhead Sheet 16059 Amount 4724. 1145 K Luttage rec'd for R.H.	Fin	QMS
	25.7.15		Rations drawn for Railhead Sheet 15925 Amount 4656. Normal Routine.	Sat	QMS
	26.7.15		Rations drawn for ESQUELBECQ — Sheet 17096 Amount 4765 to ration American Units 27 American Div. from 25th + 2 Drafts to M.T. for ARNEKE 26th + 27th — strength Amount 194	Wed	QMS
	27.7.15		Rations drawn for ESQUELBECQ — Sheet 16292 Amount 4711. For ARNEKE from Div — Sheet 2495 Amount 194	Fen	QMS
	28.7.15		Rations drawn (British American troops). Sheet 13460 Amount 4977	Sat	QMS

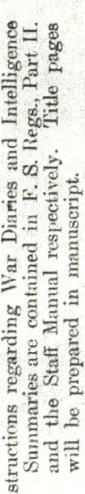

WAR DIARY

INTELLIGENCE SUMMARY

(Erase heading not required.)

Army Form C. 2118.

Place	Date	Hour	Summary of Events and Information	Weather	Remarks and references to Appendices
Sheet 27 K21 b 8.5	29.7.18		Ration dump (British + American troops) - Men 18486 Animals 4858.	Dull	DF
	30.7.18		Ration dump (British + American troops) - Men 20442 Animals 5081. Ration 4* London Scottish Rifles (fm 3rd Lanc. Div.) for one Day + on 1st Aug + on	Fine	DF
	31.7.18		Ration dump (British + American troops) - Men 19688 Animals 5026. Moved S.S.O.'s Advanced HQ	Fine	DF

[signature]
MAJOR,
S.S.O. 41st DIVISION.

WAR DIARY

INTELLIGENCE SUMMARY.

Army Form C. 2118.

Place	Date	Hour	Summary of Events and Information	Remarks and references to Appendices
1.8.18.	Mar 27 K.21	6.35	Ration drawn for British + American Troops for ESQUELBECQ - Men 19859 Animals 5018. Feed 150 A.F.A. Bde ans. 3rd Fd Amb. item. 15th Stores + 233 tons of forage for TIRQUES area - rations of tr + including rations 3rd Division with forage rations for BLENDECQUES	Fire
2.8.18.			Rations drawn for British + American Troops - Men 17294 Animals 3917	Loss
3.8.18.			Rations drawn for British + American Troops - Men 17555 Animals 3915 Issue of Biscuit fruit rifles for latter times - extra fodder En ml.	Loss
4.8.18.			Rations drawn for British + American Troops - Men 17343 Animals 3880.	Still
5.8.18.			Rations drawn for British + American Troops - Men 16569 Animals 3819	Still
6.8.18.			Rations drawn for British + American Troops - Men 17108 Animals 3830. Heavy Rain.	Still
7.8.18.			Rations drawn for British + American Troops - Men 17664 Animals 3948. 233 tes R.E. rations + requires rations ans. God + B.	Fine
8.8.18.			Rations drawn for British + American Troops - Men 17235 Animals 3947	Aust.
9.8.18.			Rations drawn for British + American Troops - Men 19232 Animals 3895. As 15th Hvy Arty rations not made for this area. 9" as ship as sp rations for this + Rockcloud Water	Still
10.8.18.			Rations drawn for British + American Troops - Men 17315 Animals 3929. Heavy Rain.	Fine
11.8.18.			Rations drawn for British + American Troops - Men 16933 Animals 3911. Issue Rations 3/168 lbs (August) less 1 oz for 124 lbs of can 13th to 21/107 of (canteen) for 123 lbs for cor 131st (August) Officers Rations of are not rationed for 12th inst.	Fine

WAR DIARY

INTELLIGENCE SUMMARY.

(Erase heading not required.)

Army Form C. 2118.

Place	Date	Hour	Summary of Events and Information	WEATHER	Remarks and references to Appendices
Sheet 27A R.21.b.9.5	12.8.18		Ration train for R.S.O. ESQUELBECQ for British American troops. Men 16725 Animals 3916. Running by M.G. 13/105 Lt. (American) join 124 US & rejoin with 13th 104 Nurses U.S. Lt. Bat. rejoin 106 Div. US M.C. 696. Total 124 US Relay M.G. to regain rations fo car. 154. Ani. 150. American R.E. Ration service never got punctual. Survey.	Fine	
"	13.8.18		Ration train for R.S.O. ESQUELBECQ for British & American troops. Men 16804 Animals 3938	Fine	
"	14.8.18		Ration train for R.S.O. ESQUELBECQ for British & American troops. Men 16714 Animals 3936	Fine	
"	15.8.18		Ration train for R.S.O. ESQUELBECQ for British & American troops. Men 16765 Animals 3937	Fine	
"	16.8.18		Ration train for R.S.O. ESQUELBECQ for British & American troops. Men 16631 Animals 3945	Fine	
"	17.8.18		Ration train for R.S.O. ESQUELBECQ for British & American troops. Men 16671 Animals 3929	Fine	
"	18.8.18		Ration train for R.S.O. ESQUELBECQ for British & American troops. Men 16568 Animals 3934	Fine	
"	19.8.18		Ration train for R.S.O. ESQUELBECQ. Men 14185 Animals 3624. Field American Bn. to 27th American Divn. for last time. con 20th Lt Yard 66 D.A. Tcar. 22nd & A.	Dull	
"	20.8.18		Ration train for R.S.O. ESQUELBECQ - Men 16331 Animals 5849.	Dull	
"	21.8.18		Ration train for R.S.O. ESQUELBECQ - Men 16298 Animals 5626	Fine	
"	22.8.18		Ration train for R.S.O. ESQUELBECQ - Men 16274 Congrats 5443. 1590 to Front Sheet requested and dispatched without new rail stations 23.8.18.	Fine	
"	23.8.18		Ration train for R.S.O. ESQUELBECQ - Men 16721 Animals 5645	Dull	
"	24.8.18		Ration train for R.S.O. ESQUELBECQ - Men 16602 Animals 5640	Wet	

Army Form C. 2118.

WAR DIARY

INTELLIGENCE SUMMARY.

(Erase heading not required.)

Place	Date	Hour	Summary of Events and Information	Remarks and references to Appendices
Abbé 21 K21	6.8.15 – 23.8.15		Rations drawn from R.S.O. ESQUELBECQ – Sheet No.462 Arrival 5771.	
	26.8.15		Rations drawn from R.S.O. ESQUELBECQ – Sheet 16313 Arrival 5744	
	27.8.18		Rations drawn from R.S.O. ESQUELBECQ – Sheet 16317 Arrival 5611	
	28.8.18		Rations drawn from R.S.O. ESQUELBECQ – Sheet 15936 Arrival 5665 – slight fog at RENESCURE Relief of Divan/Convoys. 122 J.B. Lorry one to ESQUERDES	
WIZERNES	29.8.15		Rations drawn from R.S.O. ESQUELBECQ Sheet 15854 Arrival 5611. T.H.Q. move the space required 123 J.B. Lorry one in route to ST-MARTIN-AU-LAERT Area. These Convoys take over etc to A.S.D. of 34th Division	
	30.8.15		Rations drawn from R.S.O. ESQUELBECQ Sheet 15936 Arrival 5500 from 66th D.A. for loads taken history landing	
	31.8.15		Railhead change to LUMBRES – Rations drawn from 11380 Arrival 1799 41st D.T. A.D. 34th Div lorry and retained to letter 124 JB. Lorry drawn from park of 34 JBus while 102 29 Bde lorry drawn from park of 41st Division 122 – 123 JB - drawn by H.T.	

P.C. Powis
Major,
S.S.O. 41st DIVISION.

WAR DIARY
or
INTELLIGENCE SUMMARY.
(Erase heading not required.)

Army Form C. 2118.

Instructions regarding War Diaries and Intelligence Summaries are contained in F.S. Regs., Part II. and the Staff Manual respectively. Title pages will be prepared in manuscript.

Place	Date	Hour	Summary of Events and Information	Remarks and references to Appendices
WIZERNES	1.9.18		Rations drawn for LUMBRES by M.T. Men 11,616 Animals 1630. Div: moved up from rest to ABEELE Area	Fine / P.A.P
"	2.9.18		Rations drawn from LUMBRES by M.T. Men 12,286 Animals 1913 (Reduced 2 days rations for Westleys of M.G.B.)	Dull / P.A.P
K.24.A.9.8	3.9.18		Rations drawn from LUMBRES by M.T. Men 12,066 Animals 1822 Train Headqrs. arrived from WIZERNES & arrived at K.24.A.9.8 midday	Fine / P.A.P
"	4.9.18		Rations drawn from LUMBRES by M.T. Men 11,584 Animals 1779 (Divl Troops rations drawn from ESQUELBECQ by M.T. Men 2192 Animals 1884	Dull / P.A.P
"	5.9.18		Rations drawn from ESQUELBECQ for WINNIZEELE by M.T. Men 14,897 Animals 4618. 11th Bde HFA included in ration strength of 41 Div Troops	Fine / P.A.P
"	6.9.18		Rations drawn from ESQUELBECQ for WINNIZEELE by M.T. Men 13,611 Animals 4681	Fine / P.A.P
"	7.9.18		Rations drawn from WIPPENHOEK by M.T. Men 14,785 Animals 4638	Heavy Thunder Showers / P.A.P
"	8.9.18		Rations drawn from WIPPENHOEK by H.T. Men 14,750 Animals 4661	Wet / P.A.P
"	9.9.18		Rations drawn from WIPPENHOEK by H.T. Men 14,569 Animals 4721	Wet / P.A.P
"	10.9.18		Rations drawn from WIPPENHOEK by M.T. Men 14,788 Animals 4651	Wet / P.A.P

Army Form C. 2118.

WAR DIARY
or
INTELLIGENCE SUMMARY.
(Erase heading not required.)

Instructions regarding War Diaries and Intelligence Summaries are contained in F. S. Regs., Part II. and the Staff Manual respectively. Title pages will be prepared in manuscript.

Place	Date	Hour	Summary of Events and Information	weather	Remarks and references to Appendices
K.24.A.9.B	11.9.18		Rations drawn from NIPPENHOEK by H.T. Men 15045 Animals 4638	wet	W.D.W.
"	12.9.18		Rations drawn from NIPPENHOEK by H.T. Men 14953 Animals 4658	wet	W.D.W.
"	13.9.18		Rations drawn from NIPPENHOEK by H.T. Men 14853 Animals 4630	wet	W.D.W.
"	14.9.18		Rations drawn from WIPPENHOEK by H.T. Men 14959 Animals 4636	Fine	W.D.W.
"	15.9.18		Rations drawn from WIPPENHOEK by H.T. Men 14823 Animals 4634	Fine	W.D.W.
"	16.9.18		Rations drawn from NIPPENHOEK by H.T. Men 12,401 Animals 4371. Area then rations being drawn from 29' Div Pack, commencing 16'.	Fine	124 Bdes in Back truck W.D.W.
"	17.9.18		Rations drawn from WIPPENHOEK by H.T. Men 12195 Animals 4475	Fine	W.D.W.
"	18.9.18		Rations drawn from WIPPENHOEK by H.T. Men 12211 Animals 4385	Fine	W.D.W.
"	19.9.18		Rations drawn from WIPPENHOEK by H.T. Men 12243 Animals 4393	Fine	W.D.W.
"	20.9.18		Sec. orders to 11th A.F.A. Bde. 1 day Res. for an. 22 lb for boot line, also 41st T.M.S.R.A. Sent 1 days Res. for attack 1 Div. and 41st T.M.T. log. at STEENVOORDE 24'. Sheet Roo H.D.3 Anchels H.D. 399, L.D. 3290.	Fine	W.D.W.
"	21.9.18		Rations drawn from WIPPENHOEK by H.T. Men 11036 Animals 3462	Wet	W.D.W.
"	22.9.18		Rations drawn from WIPPENHOEK by H.T. Men 11069 Animals 3468. WATTEN by M.T. for 124 I.B. Group - Men 2724 Animals 252	Fine	W.D.W.

WAR DIARY
INTELLIGENCE SUMMARY.
(Erase heading not required.)

Army Form C. 2118.

Place	Date	Hour	Summary of Events and Information	Weather	Remarks and references to Appendices
K.24.a.9.8.	23.9.18		Draw for WIPPENHOEK by H.T. Iss. 10850 " " WATTEN by M.T. for 124 S.B. Group - Iss. 2517 Amout 3464 Amout 249	Fine	W.D.M.
"	24.9.18		Draw for WIPPENHOEK by H.T. Iss. 11249 Amout 3490 " " WATTEN by M.T. for 124 S.B. Group - Iss. 2389 Amout 264	Fine	W.D.M.
"	25.9.18		Draw for WIPPENHOEK by H.T. Iss. 11469 Amout 3547 " " WATTEN by M.T. for 124 S.B. Group - Iss. 2585 Amout 255	Wet	W.D.M.
"	26.9.18		Draw by H.T. for WIPPENHOEK (+M.T. for 124 S.B.) Iss. 14059 Amout 3864	Dull	W.D.M.
DALLINGTON CAMP M.27.c.29.c.8.2 - 27.9.18	27.9.18		T.H.Q. move to New augment ment Station down for this day for WIPPENHOEK by H.T. Iss. 14155 Amout 3947. (This Quota - 50 H.T. +150 L.D. for Reserve Sup) 10468 from Lorries in this area.	Fine	W.D.M.
M.25 C.23.b.8.4 28.9.18 (Reserve Camp)	28.9.18		Ration drawn by H.T. for WIPPENHOEK - Iss. 15274 (includes 1000 suff. for the Reafus Camp) Amout 3822 now to be made augment ment	Dull	W.D.M.
"	29.9.18		Load of M.T. for Reserve Sup drawing balance of Iss. Rns + Engines for R.S.O. WIPPENHOEK - tied I Iss. Rns 14915 Amout 3792 Office Sations. M.T. took Pty again for W'HOEK. and pack loaded. delivery morning of Sept 30 - Iss. 14965 Amout 3797	Fine	W.D.M.
Do.	30.9.18		Railhead changes to VLAMERTINGHE. Drawn by M.T. (Lorries delivered morning of Oct 1.) Iss. Rns 14817 Amout 3809	Very Wet	W.D.M.

E.J.Maile Capt.

WAR DIARY

INTELLIGENCE SUMMARY.
(Erase heading not required.)

Army Form C. 2118.

Instructions regarding War Diaries and Intelligence Summaries are contained in F.S. Regs., Part II. and the Staff Manual respectively. Title pages will be prepared in manuscript.

Place	Date	Hour	Summary of Events and Information	Remarks and references to Appendices
At 28/G.23.B.S.4 (Dornan bang)	1.10.18		Rations drawn by M.T. for VLAMERTINGHE (to to Dumps lorries) Jun 14,393 Animals 3870. 4½a T.M. Bde return Brit for cav Voir 3rd Adv Div Reception bay. Sty 3rd Cav & Div Ration to draw rations above Opre R.S.O. WIPPENHOEK car 4 & a	Fine
do	2.10.18		Rations drawn by M.T. for VLAMERTINGHE (to be dumped lorries) Men 13260 Animals 3778.	Dull
do	3.10.18		Rations drawn by M.T. for VLAMERTINGHE (to be dumped lorries). Men 11950. Animals 3855.	Fine
At 28/I.26.c.3.3 4.10.18 (Oakhof Camp)	4.10.18		T.H.Q. move to place marquee camp. Drew for VLAMERTINGHE – Jun Jen 15021 Animals 5268. Ration 101st Bn. M.G.C. 2nd 3rd C.A. ; Col XI Anz Bde R.F.A.	Dec
do	5.10.18		Rations drawn for VLAMERTINGHE – Men 14120 Animals 4991	Fine
do	6.10.18		Rations drawn for VLAMERTINGHE – Men 15363 Animals 4852. 122 JS. am to BUSSEBOOM area.	Fine
do	7.10.18		1st ration 150 Indian (with A&C 6) for car 7th & 11 Rations drawn for Railhead – Men 14095 Animals 4975. Jn. 1050 Indian Ref. (C.C. Bu scale subf) of 180	Fine
do	8.10.18		Rations drawn – Jun 14271 Animals 4907	Fine
do	9.10.18		Rations drawn – Jun 15317 Animals 4922	Fine
do	10.10.18		Rations drawn for R.S.O. VLAMERTINGHE – Jun 15730 Animals 4933	Fine
do	11.10.18		Rations drawn – Jun 15601 Animals 4799 (includes rations for Div Recept bay car 12th & 13th Nov.) Ration + forage of 122 JS. + 124 JS. (Cav 13th) Cav Dumps and Heffl j School Jun 1312 Group to draw to H.T. & 012 for VLAMERTINGHE for car 13th	Bull
do	12.10.18		Rations drawn for Railhead – Jun 14916 Animals 4825	Nic
do	13.10.18		122 JS. drew rations for 6 times Batty for car 14th. My Jun 2120 Animals 243 (by M.T.) drew for VLAM – Jun Cav 15211. Animals 4792 (includes 122 JS. car 15th) – All of M.T. except 124 JS. + Indian Ration 1043.	Dec

WAR DIARY

INTELLIGENCE SUMMARY

(Erase heading not required.)

Army Form C. 2118.

Place	Date	Hour	Summary of Events and Information	Weather	Remarks and references to Appendices
LANKHOF CAMP C1.23/ 126 C1.23	14.10.18		Railhead changed to TROIS ROIS. Ration to draw by M.T. partly for S.T., S.T.(2) 122 W3 123 W3 dumps with others and all groups, dumps for [Railhead by] H.T. Rations drawn from Jan 15360. Amount 4715.	Fine	Q.P.
"	15.10.18		Drawn from Railhead – Then: rations - 18407. Amount Rs. 4729. Horse Rations.	Fine	Q.P.
"	16.10.18		Railways drawn from THREE KINGS to H.T. – Then 15976. Amount 4698. Return J.H.Q. rations to DADIZEELE	Very Foggy	Q.P.
DADIZEELE	17.10.18		Rations drawn by Railhead – Then: 13990. Amount 4706. All drawn by rifle to registration of DADIZEELE Rail-M.T. load of Rations day and again deliver to station. Also Hoogha Relief Pas for R.S.O. YLAMERTINGHE for 119a and J.rocd.		Q.P.
"	18.10.18		Rations drawn by M.T. gathering afternoon in Reserve Dump. Then 12709. Amount 3770. Half of the Dump numbered, balance with rations drawn for Railhead (Issues – Then 13740 Amount 4693). dumped with cart loads of the Supplies Bread + room 1500 rations for officers on outpost.	Dull	Q.P.
"	19.10.18		Drawn from R'Ed + dumped as usual – Then: R. 13287. Amount 4656. Also S.T. Ration for troops down S.Rile. + count.		Q.P.
"	G.H.C.B.3 20.10.18		Drawn from Railhead – Then: Rn. 15585. Amount 4737. Also Ration for Indian 937. Issue to Divn. marginally 1000 Burlari Rations drawn for troops.	Rain	Q.P.
BISSEGHEM	21.10.18		Railn. drawn for Railhead – Then 15111. Amounts 4790. Divn. H.Q. move to BISSEGHEM. 1000 burlari Rations drawn for troops	Rain	Q.P.
"	22.10.18		Railhead changed to LEDEGHEM. Ration drawn – Then 15132. Amounts 5118. 4000 burlari Rations drawn for troops.	Rain	Q.P.
"	23.10.18		Rations drawn for Railhead – Then 14900 Amounts 4593. 8000 burlari Rations drawn for troops. Path Train last had to send carrys for all cuts	Fine	Q.P.
"	24.10.18		Ration drawn for Railway – Then 14959. Amount 4980. 8000 burlari Rations drawn for troops	Fine	Q.P.
"	25.10.18		Ration drawn from Railway – Then 14186. Amount 4773. 12000 burlari Rations drawn for troops. Lorries just loaded songs are not about to army	Fine	Q.P.

A.534. Wt.W4973/M687 750,000 8/16 D.D.&L. Ltd. Forms/C.2118/13.

Army Form C. 2118.

WAR DIARY
INTELLIGENCE SUMMARY
(Erase heading not required.)

Instructions regarding War Diaries and Intelligence Summaries are contained in F.S. Regs., Part II. and the Staff Manual respectively. Title pages will be prepared in manuscript.

Place	Date	Hour	Summary of Events and Information	Weather	Remarks and references to Appendices
BISSEGHEM	26.10.18.		Ration draw for LEDEGHEM by M.T. and despatched. 23 horses — Men 1360. Animals 4974	Fine	O.C
			Issued burying Ration men for Traction		
"	27.10.18		Draw by H.T. Men Ration 14603 (Includes 1 day for Div Recepln camp) Animals 4932	Dull	O.C
			Indian Ration drawn 982 (On own supply) also 32000 burying Ration for Traction		
	28.10.18		Draw by H.T. again today — Men Ration 14097 Animals 4880 — also 20000 burying Ration for Traction	Fine	O.C
COURTRAI (N2b3.9)	29.10.18		Move to place marquees road Rations change to BISSEGHEM. Train ran late.	Fine	O.C
			Ration drawn by H.T. Men 14823 Animals 4842		
	30.10.18		Ration drawn by H.T. Men 13093 Animals 4815	Fine	O.C
	31.10.18		Ration drawn by H.T. Men 14242 Animals 4853	Dull	O.C

MAJOR,
S.S.O. 41ST DIVISION.

WAR DIARY
INTELLIGENCE SUMMARY
(Erase heading not required.)

Army Form C. 2118.

Place	Date	Hour	Summary of Events and Information		Remarks and references to Appendices
COURTRAI (29/N2&3 8)	1/11/15		Due draw by H.T. except 123 + 124 S/S, who draw by M.T. Pack train any lost. Ration drawn Jan. 13591. Annual 4795.	Fine	PM P
SWEVEGHEM (29/O1&3 8)	2/11/15		Some of Horse nosebags issued. 3 Bde Gp to draw by H.T. and S.P.s by M.T. Ration (Corn + Hail) 13710. Annual 4795.	Dull	PM P
"	3.11.15		Ration drawn Jan. 13920. Annual 4801 also gpl Ration for Indian Horse Routine.	Dull	PM P
"	4.11.15		Ration drawn Jan. 14495. Annual 4791. Horse Routine. Receiving all P.M. stores for Railhead.	Fine	PM P
ESSCHER (34/J32 b11)	5.11.15		Some of Horse nosebags issued. Routine draw – Jan. 13988. Annual 4786.	Very Wet	PM P
"	6.11.15		Ration drawn for Railhead – Jan. 13227. Annual 5645 (includes for am 7" + 8". XI" A.F.A. Btn) Am Group draw by M.T. except 122 S/S who draw by H.T.	Very Wet	PM P
"	7.11.15		Some of Horse nosebags issued – 3 Bde Gp V. draw by H.T. + S.P.s by M.T. Ration drawn – Jan. 14485. Anuls 4743.	Dull	PM P
"	8.11.15		All gps – draw by M.T. Res drawn Jan. 14239. Annual 4740. Horse Routine.	Dull	PM P
"	9.11.15		Railhead changed to VICHTE – all ration drawn by H.T. – Jan. 14379. Annual 4720. Pack train only issue.	Fine	PM P
M.29/I57 d.9, M.1ooh.h."	10.11.15		Some of Hard nosebags issued. All ration drawn by M.T. Jan. 13870. Annual 4578, also note for Pack train late 9.30p. Iss. 11" Scottish Howitzer Bty, con. 11" mid.	Fine	PM P
M.30 M.4 d.9	11.11.15		Some of Horse nosebags issued. Ration will drawn by M.T. Jan. 13867. Annual 4581. Ration all draw by B.T. 123 S/S 124 S/S etc	Fine	PM P
"	12.11.15		Jam ration in gratis – Meals draw Jan. 13552. Annual 4573	Fine	
"	13.11.15		Ration for gratis. Ration drawn Jan. 14257. Annual 4579 xxxxxxx 14½ xxx	Fine	PM P

WAR DIARY
INTELLIGENCE SUMMARY
(Erase heading not required.)

Army Form C. 2118.

Place	Date	Hour	Summary of Events and Information	Weather	Remarks and references to Appendices
NEDERBRAKEL Billet 36	14.11.18		Draw to place marquee & erect. Ration drawn - Iss. 14078 Arrears A362	Fine	PP
	15.11.18		M.T. able to carry supplies and all supplies changed at NEDERBRAKEL	Fine	PP
			Routine as yesterday. Ration drawn - Iss. 13418 Arrears 4704		
	16.11.18		Routine as yesterday. Ration drawn - Iss. 14750 Rations 28 of 1st reinforcements) Arrears 4575. Issue 11 Jackets Drayton Bristol car "17" + n. Case drew for Rations 3rd reinfor- received. O.P. of N. and arrears.	Fine	PP
	17.11.18		Rations drawn for Rations Iss. 13862 Arrears 4436 also for Indents 952. bus car groups for today at Railhead Station	Fine	PP
Billet 701 SANTBERGEN	18.11.18		Division continues march to Germany. T.H.Q moves to SANTBERGEN. All ration drawn by M.T. Iss. 14033 Arrears 4746	Wet	PP
do	19.11.18		Routine as yesterday. Ration drawn - Iss. 13603 Arrears 4673 It has been arranged to now relay of horses & Lorries for supplying army to keep ahead	Fine	PP
do	20.11.18		Railwar changed to OUDENARDE. Ration drawn Iss. 13680 Arrears 4431	Fine	PP
do	21.11.18		Draw from Point of 9th Div at VICHTE on 21st + 22nd ukeless. 9 Div drew to 41. Div Park at OUDENARDE Rations of H.Q Div acting in charge of VICHTE on 22nd inst. Ration drawn I Iss. 13677 Arrears 4326 about to return to Indents O.P. Arrears in position to 27 ADAMSTRAAT GRAMMONT.	Fine	PP
27 ADAMSTRAAT GRAMMONT.	22.11.18		Park sections late Rations drawn - Iss. 13279 Arrears A305	Fine	PP

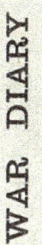

Army Form C. 2118.

WAR DIARY
or
INTELLIGENCE SUMMARY.
(Erase heading not required.)

Instructions regarding War Diaries and Intelligence Summaries are contained in F. S. Regs., Part II. and the Staff Manual respectively. Title pages will be prepared in manuscript.

Place	Date	Hour	Summary of Events and Information	Remarks and references to Appendices
ADAMSTRAAT GRAMMONT.	23.11.18		Railhead change to HERSEAUX - Ration drawn Jhn 13834 Animals 4394	
do	24.11.18		Ration drawn in Rankhead - Jhn 13389 Horses 4380 also 1008 ratns for Indian	
do	25.11.18		Ration drawn - Jhn 13087 Animals 4285 - Horse Ration	
do	26.11.18		Ration drawn - Jhn 13102 Animals 4264 Horse Ration	
do	27.11.18		Horse Ration - Ration drawn for Rainhera - Jhn 13305 Animals 4378	
do	28.11.18		Railhead change to TOURNAI - Rations drawn - Jhn 13075 Animals 4373 - Feed 186 total by ca 29th 4 Jr.	
do	29.11.18		Ration drawn for Rankhead - Jhn 14126 Animals 4329 (inclusive ca of 29" & 30" Feed for 186 Indns)	
do	30.11.18		Ration drawn for Cavalna - Jhn 14099 Animals 4344 Feed 186 total by last line exemption. See 1.	

Army Form C. 2118.

WAR DIARY
INTELLIGENCE SUMMARY.
(Erase heading not required.)

Instructions regarding War Diaries and Intelligence Summaries are contained in F. S. Regs., Part II. and the Staff Manual respectively. Title pages will be prepared in manuscript.

Place	Date	Hour	Summary of Events and Information	Weather	Remarks and references to Appendices
27 ADAMSTRAAT GRAMMONT	1-12-18		Rations drawn from TOURNAI by M.T. Ser. 12622 Arrivals 4308 also 1008 rations for Indians	Fine	
"	2-12-18		Rations drawn for Rastons Ser. 12938 - Arrivals 4295. Horses Routine	Wet	
"	3-12-18		Drawn for Rations - Ser. Rations 13066 Arrivals 4307	Wet	
"	4-12-18		Drawn for Rations - Ser. Rations 15947 (includes rations rum 3rm & 6th for aftermovement 1500 reinforcements) Horses Routine.	Wet	
"	5-12-18		Rations Change to GHISLENGHIEN. Rations drawn Ser. 14376 Arrivals 4302 Horse Routine.	Dull	
"	6-12-18		Drew again from GHISLENGHIEN - Rations drawn - Ser. 14313 Arrivals 4304	Fine	
"	7-12-18		Rations as yesterday - Rations drawn Ser. 14285 Arrivals 4302	Fine	
"	8-12-18		Horse Routine. Rations drawn - Ser. 14444 Rations 4291 also 1008 rations for Indians.	Fine	
"	9-12-18		Rations as yesterday - Rations drawn Ser. 14309, Arrivals 4324	Fine	
"	10-12-18		Horse Routine - Rations drawn Ser. 14377 Arrivals 4305	Wet	
"	11-12-18		Rations drawn - Ser. 14303 Arrivals 4291. Division re-grouped into 5 groups of 4 brigades. Orders to arrange for accom. of am. Fuel Res. Coy. 67 15 pdr. these supporting Reld front supplies Coy of 11/67 with fuel all arrived. We are going early with full fuel etc. transported Motor lor.	Wet	
ENGHIEN.	12-12-18		Ser. & So. 4 Rue de station - ENGHIEN. Railhead changes to BRAIN LE COMTE. Rations drawn - Ser. 14311 Arrivals 4329	Wet	

WAR DIARY
INTELLIGENCE SUMMARY
(Erase heading not required.)

Army Form C. 2118.

Instructions regarding War Diaries and Intelligence Summaries are contained in F. S. Regs., Part II. and the Staff Manual respectively. Title pages will be prepared in manuscript.

Place	Date	Hour	Summary of Events and Information	Weather	Remarks and references to Appendices
HAL	13.12.18		Route Brigade - Rue 15 7 Rue de Bolton, HAL. Ration draw Sur 14372 Arrivals 4232. Pack train very late	Fair	
BRAINE L'ALLEUD	14.12.18		Sur 15 Hour marginale route - Ration draw Sur 14277 Arrivals 4264.	Fair	
	15.12.18		Parties to gather info. King "E" & Queen did not move. Park train arrived at midway - Ration draw Sur 14295 Arrivals 4294 also 1015 rations for Ichen 3200	Fine	
	16.12.18		Brigade to move forward again - Ration draw Sur 14269 Arrivals 4253	Fine	
MARBAIS (Vic Rue du Prisonnier)	17.12.18		Rose to Hour marginale Chaseur. Ration draw Sur 14021 Arrivals 4274	Dec	
MAZY	18.12.18		Sur 16 Hour marginale arrived. Packet changes to GEMBLOUX, Pack train due 17th did not arrive. with 18th as usn to E GEMBLOUX. Ration draw Sur 14070 4252 (some R'ts 15th)	Dec	
WARET la CHAUSSÉE	19.12.18		Sur 16 Hour marginale route - Ration draw Sur 14272 Arrivals 4252	Dec	
HUY	20.12.18		Sur 16 Hour marginale arrived - Ration draw Sur 14404 Arrivals 4253 - Pack train arrived to draw very late	Nov	
HUY	21.12.18		Pack train did not arrive Ordre - 22 trips late - Ration draw Sur 14212 Arrivals 4249	Fine	
	22.12.18		Sure first 4 rate trips to Klusen de Luje - Ration draw Sur 13831 Arrivals 4248 also 1018 Ration for Indian	Fine	
	23.12.18		Ration draw Sur 13900 Arrivals 4253. All suffices no motor by H.T.	Dec	
	24.12.18		Ration draw - Sur 13735 Arrivals 4295. Train was late	Dec	
	25.12.18		Ration draw - Sur 13865 Arrivals 4284 train late	Fine	
	26.12.18		Ration draw - Sur 14141 Arrivals 4327. Ind Advanced H.Q. Aeroplane Service hill R.A./T. 28th 28th & 61	Fine	

Army Form C. 2118.

WAR DIARY
or
INTELLIGENCE SUMMARY

(Erase heading not required.)

Instructions regarding War Diaries and Intelligence Summaries are contained in F.S. Regs., Part II. and the Staff Manual respectively. Title pages will be prepared in manuscript.

Place	Date	Hour	Summary of Events and Information		Remarks and references to Appendices
HQ.	27.12.15		Rations drawn for Rothven - Iner. 13775 Amounts 4294. Rations still about 24 hrs behind time.	Weather Bitter	SgtF
	28.12.15		Rain from dawn 25th amour. Rations 15.30 hrs 29th inst. Rations drawn Iner. 13635 Amounts 4274.	Wet.	JS
	29.12.15		Poor train still about 24 hrs late - Rations drawn - Iner. 13566 Amount 4265. Also 108 rations for Indians	Wet	RS
	30.12.15		Rations drawn as Rothven - Iner. 13511. Amount 4264. Bacon issued in lieu Margarine	Wet	RS
	31.12.15		Rations drawn for Rothven Iner. 13641 Amounts 4360. No Margarine or Saguersaut available. Rated 75th Lusty Inf. on Jan 2nd + on the battle ever for Scotic Issue since of RSO HQ on Dec 31st Jan 1.	Fine	SgtF

C. Pratt
Capt. SO. 24 per Division

D. D. & L., London, L.C.
(10340) Wt W3300/P713 750,000 1/15 E 2688 Forms/C2115/16

Army Form C. 2118.

WAR DIARY
of
INTELLIGENCE SUMMARY.
(Erase heading not required.)

Instructions regarding War Diaries and Intelligence Summaries are contained in F. S. Regs., Part II. and the Staff Manual respectively. Title pages will be prepared in manuscript.

Place	Date	Hour	Summary of Events and Information	Remarks and references to Appendices
HUY	1.1.19		Ration drawn from Railhead – Men 13687 Animals 4260. Park train sides report 24 hrs late	Fine
	2.1.19		Ration drawn – Men 13689 Animals 4262. M.V issued in lieu Margarine	Fine
	3.1.19		Ration drawn from HUY Railhead – Men 16632 Animals 4464 – Men attached to 199th Inf Bde of 66th Div also drawn if (Rosieres Park (Brown)) fr issue 3.1 – + rations (Bacon issued in lieu Margarine)	Fine
	4.1.19		Previous Ration drawn – Men 17786 Animals 4618. Also 17th the issue supply actually from Rosieres Park	Fair
	5.1.19		Ration train – Men 17872 Animals 4612. Also ration (extra) drawn fr entraining troops (fr 124 fr 183 } 4164 Animals 2065 hard rations	Ration change to SAMPS IN 6.1.19 Fair
	6.1.19		Ration ration (hard) drawn fr entraining troops – 1440 + 322 Animals Fed Canadian units as they pulled Canadian fr. 9th Brit 41 Bde Park as they were in Samps. Ration drawn for Park due to arrive Railhead 6th – Men 17981 Animals 4656	Fair
	7.1.19		Both day's ration drawn for entraining troops – Men 1828 Animals 190 Ration drawn fr Park due Railhead 7th Jan – Men 18112 Animals 4388	Fine Iron rat'n issue
	8.1.19		Ration drawn for entraining troops – Men 1855 Animals 252. Ration (drawn off Park) due Railhead 8th inst – Men 18448 Animals 4734	Fine
	9.1.19		Ration day ration drawn for entraining troops – Men 1371 Animals 257. Ration drawn off Park day Railhead 9th – Men 18354 Animals 4725. Train stuck up late	Fine
	10.1.19		Ration day ration drawn for entraining troops – Men 1221 Animals 385. Ration deliver D.D.&L.. 101 (artillery reduct 11th) – Men 14117 Animals 4712	Fine

Army Form C. 2118.

WAR DIARY
INTELLIGENCE SUMMARY.
(Erase heading not required.)

Instructions regarding War Diaries and Intelligence Summaries are contained in F.S. Regs., Part II, and the Staff Manual respectively. Title pages will be prepared in manuscript.

Place	Date	Hour	Summary of Events and Information		Remarks and references to Appendices
MARIENBURG 5th Reinforcement COLOGNE	10.1.19		T.H.Q. - open to three new army areas — Railhead & stores by train ROSRATH.	Fine	
"	11.1.19		Ration train Jun 13695 Arrives 4533		
"	12.1.19		Ration train for Railhead - Jun 13322 Arrives 4597 Arrives	Fine	
"	13.1.19		Ration train from Railhead - Jun 14999 Arrives 4391	Fine	
"			Air leave — 8.8.30 + 123 I/3 stores by M.T. — other group to H.T.		
"	14.1.19		Ration train also here - Ration grown three 13363 Arrives 3828 - that train to Sappers 947 Ration store	Fine	
"	15.1.19		Ration train for Railhead - Jun 13725 Arrives 4610	Fine	
"	16.1.19		Ration train for ROSRATH - Jun 13979 Arrives 4499	Fine	
"	17.1.19		Ration train for ROSRATH - Jun 13592 Arrives 4576	All	
"	18.1.19		Ration train from ROSRATH - Jun 13666 - Arrives A231	All	
"	19.1.19		Ration drawn for Railhead - 739.24 Arrives A257	All	
"	20.1.19		Ration drawn for Railhead - Jun 13698 Arrives 4253	Fine	
"	21.1.19		Ration drawn for ROSRATH - Jun 13788 Arrives 4267	Fine	
"	22.1.19		Ration drawn for ROSRATH - Jun 13752 Arrives 4350 train 16153	Fine	
"	23.1.19		Ration drawn for ROSRATH - Jun 13697 Arrives 4247	Fine	
"	24.1.19		Ration drawn - Jun 13839 Arrives 4236	Fine	
"	25.1.19		Ration drawn for 2 Bn 123 I.B. - Jun 3200 Arrives 320. Some Ration drawn for Railway Construction. Jun 13525 Arrives 4235. To officers' mess for Ration train	Fine	

Army Form C. 2118.

WAR DIARY
of
INTELLIGENCE SUMMARY.
(Erase heading not required.)

Instructions regarding War Diaries and Intelligence Summaries are contained in F. S. Regs., Part II. and the Staff Manual respectively. Title pages will be prepared in manuscript.

Place	Date	Hour	Summary of Events and Information		Remarks and references to Appendices
MARIENBURG 3 Armee Korps COLOGNE	26.1.19		Hostilities change to HEUMAR. All troops drawn by H.T. Rations drawn [illegible] for party from COLOGNE Base Park. Issuing 24 war est to [illegible] on 27th inst. Rations drawn — Men 13632 Animals 17239 about 1075 Rations for sale	Gross	O.K.
do	27.1.19		Rations drawn — Men 13535 Animals 4223	ans	O.K.
do	28.1.19		Rations drawn from HEUMAR Rations — Men 13600 Animals 4225	fair	O.K.
do	29.1.19		Rations drawn from HEUMAR Rations — Men 13464 Animals 4225	fair	O.K.
do	30.1.19		Rations drawn from HEUMAR Rations — Men 13400 Animals 4218	dull	O.K.
do	31.1.19		Rations drawn from HEUMAR — Men 13125 Animals 7181 Pack [illegible] and animal normal	fair	O.K.

[signature]
MAJOR.
S.S.O. 41st DIVISION.

Army Form C. 2118.

WAR DIARY
or
INTELLIGENCE SUMMARY.
(Erase heading not required.)

Instructions regarding War Diaries and Intelligence Summaries are contained in F.S. Regs., Part II. and the Staff Manual respectively. Title pages will be prepared in manuscript.

[Stamp: SENIOR SUPPLY OFFICER / No. / Date / 41st DIVISION]

Place	Date	Hour	Summary of Events and Information	Remarks and references to Appendices
MARIENBURG Barracks School	1.2.19		Ration drawn for HEUMAR — Men 13213 Horses 7177. Carriage duty at R.10. No. 10-11 1st Train know nam	
do	2.2.19		Ration drawn from HEUMAR — Men 12848 Horses 7180 — Drew 1905 Ration for Indian Coys at first army village	
do	3.2.19		Ration drawn for CHEUMAR Hostlers — Men 12487 Horses 7156	
do	4.2.15		Ration drawn for HEUMAR — Men 12176 Horses 7141	
do	5.2.19		Ration drawn for HEUMAR — Men 12038 Horses 7126	
do	6.2.19		Ration drawn for HEUMAR — Men 11950 Horses 7157	
do	7.2.19		Ration drawn for HEUMAR — Men 12127 Horses 7131	
do	8.2.19		Ration drawn for HEUMAR — Men 11990 Horses 7080	
do	9.2.19		Ration drawn for HEUMAR — Men 11810 Horses 7128 — also 987 Ration for Indian	
do	10.2.19		Ration drawn for HEUMAR — Men 12144 Horses 7107. No ration issues	
			24 hr ration rations held until relieved or arrangements by D.A.	
do	11.2.19		Ration drawn for HEUMAR — Men 11819 Horses 7152	
do	12.2.19		Ration drawn for HEUMAR — Men 11452 Horses 7123 [Supply train for Roisdorf 953]	
do	13.2.19		Ration drawn for HEUMAR — Men 11356 Horses 7110	
do	14.2.19		Ration drawn for HEUMAR — Men 11559 Horses 7094. Ration train not yet been available	

(39475) Wt W2338/P363 500,000 12/17 D.D. & L. Sch. 52a. Forms/C2118/15.

Army Form C. 2118.

WAR DIARY
INTELLIGENCE SUMMARY.
(Erase heading not required.)

Instructions regarding War Diaries and Intelligence Summaries are contained in F. S. Regs., Part II. and the Staff Manual respectively. Title pages will be prepared in manuscript.

Place	Date	Hour	Summary of Events and Information	Weather	Remarks and references to Appendices
MARIENBURG bei CÖLN 5 Rheinprovinz COLOGNE	15.2.19		Rations drawn from HEUMAR — Men 11450. Animals 4099. Vehicles not available	Wet	
	16.2.19		Rations drawn from HEUMAR — Men 11274. Animals 4168 also 1001 Rations for Italian Prisoners. Vehicles not available — "Italian Prisoners arrived".	Wet	
	17.2.19		Rations drawn from HEUMAR — Men 11345. Animals 4095. Vehicles not available.	Wet	
	18.2.19		Rations drawn from HEUMAR — Men 11615. Animals 4100. Details still not available.	Wet	
	19.2.19		Rations drawn from HEUMAR — Men 10604 (due to moving in land) Animals 4095.	Wet	
	20.2.19		Rations drawn from HEUMAR — Men 10767. Animals 4094. Vehicles still not available.	Fine	
	21.2.19		Rations drawn from HEUMAR — Men 11069. Animals 4090. Vehicles not available.	Dull	
	22.2.19		Rations drawn from HEUMAR — Men 11077. Animals 4090. Vehicles not available.	Fine	
	23.2.19		Rations drawn from HEUMAR — Men 10920. Animals 4055. Also 994 Rations of Rations to Italians	Fine	
	24.2.19		Rations drawn from HEUMAR — Men 10994. Animals 4084. No vehicles available for day drawn	Fine	
	25.2.19		Rations drawn from HEUMAR — Men 10883. Animals 4061 Near Prisoners released day 25th/26th their Regt P.S. Packet present in Camp — Coy D/S. Mails to Army H/Q. Vehicles not available.		
	26.2.19		Rations drawn from HEUMAR — Men 11030. Animals 4176. Yr Dismvd available. Draft antryes from to Snr. Res. Bn. Unit 13-10-8 Sty. 113. 82. 72. 11th Musketeers Drawn for (5th Bn) minus R. Ser. 27. 21.? (Vedra)		Wells
	27.2.19		Rations drawn from HEUMAR — Men 10758. Animals 3980. Vehicles not available. 18th K.R.R. Drawn for 2nd Sur. Relieve Gar. 25. (20th D.L.I.) — 28. — 23rd R. Sur. 3rd Sur. available 4th Sur. 5th Sur. 1st	Wet	Wells

Army Form C. 2118.

WAR DIARY
INTELLIGENCE SUMMARY.
(Erase heading not required.)

Instructions regarding War Diaries and Intelligence Summaries are contained in F. S. Regs., Part II. and the Staff Manual respectively. Title pages will be prepared in manuscript.

Place	Date	Hour	Summary of Events and Information	Remarks and references to Appendices
MARIENBURG	25.2.19		Ration drawn from HEUMAR Rathaus – Men 10342 Animals 4073. Issue not available	

WAR DIARY
INTELLIGENCE SUMMARY.
(Erase heading not required.)

Army Form C. 2118.

Place	Date	Hour	Summary of Events and Information	Weather	Remarks and references to Appendices
MARIEN BURG & Beginning Section (CO-OG)	1.3.19		Rations drawn for HEUMAR - Men 10,225 Animals 4,062. Rations not available	Fine	WSM
	2.3.19		Rations drawn Men 10326 Animals 4037 also rations for 1058 Indian	Fine	WSM
—	2.3.19		Rations drawn for HEUMAR - Men 10508 Animals 4031	Fair	WSM
„	4.3.19		Rations drawn for HEUMAR - Men 12641 Animals 4030 (Indian rations for 53rd Divn. 4" 5" 6" this date. [716 army] arrived late "own night rations rations)	Rain	WSM
	5.3.19		Rations drawn for HEUMAR - Men 11670 Animals 4032	Fair	WSM
	6.3.19		Rations drawn for HEUMAR Rations - Men 11239 Animals 4017 9th E. Surreys Divn rations for an 5th- 6t rations for 12th E. Surrey.	Fair	WSM
	7.3.19		Rations drawn - Men 11810 Animals 4023	Fair	WSM
	8.3.19		Rations drawn from HEUMAR - Men 11519 Animals 4025	Fair	WSM
	9.3.19		Rations drawn from HEUMAR - Men 11321 Animals 4021, also 1043 rations for Indian	Fine	WSM
	10.3.19		Rations drawn for HEUMAR - Men 11363 Animals 4022	Fair	WSM
	11.3.19		Rations drawn from HEUMAR - Men 11674 Animals 4018	Fine	WSM
	12.3.19		Rations drawn for HEUMAR - Men 11333 Animals 4007	Fine	WSM
	13.3.19		Rations drawn for HEUMAR - Men 11485 Animals 3999	Fair	WSM
„	14.3.19		Rations drawn from HEUMAR - Men 11157 Animals 3965	Fine	WSM

Army Form C. 2118.

WAR DIARY
INTELLIGENCE SUMMARY.
(Erase heading not required)

Instructions regarding War Diaries and Intelligence Summaries are contained in F. S. Regs., Part II. and the Staff Manual respectively. Title pages will be prepared in manuscript.

Place	Date	Hour	Summary of Events and Information	Remarks and references to Appendices
MARIENBURG 5 Kiometres South of COLOGNE.	15.3.19		Ration train from HEUMAR. Recruits - Men 11359. Animals 3969. No cavalry available. Major P.D. Protheroe returned from leave and reassumes duties. Sec. of Div. changed to train Division.	
"	16.3.19		Ration train for HEUMAR. Rations - Men 11343. Animals 3977 also rations for 1008 Indians. No trouble available	
"	17.3.19		Ration train for HEUMAR - Men 11327. Animals 3990.	
"	18.3.19		Ration train for HEUMAR - Men 11181. Animals 3987.	
"	19.3.19		Ration train for HEUMAR - Men 11498. Animals 4177.	
"	20.3.19		Ration train for HEUMAR - Men 11368. Animals 4057.	
"	21.3.19		Ration train for HEUMAR - Men 11650. Animals 4194. Horse Rations.	
"	22.3.19		Ration train for HEUMAR. Rations - Men 11429. Animals 4136.	
"	23.3.19		Ration train for HEUMAR. Rations - Men 11325. Animals 4035, also rations for 1015 Indians.	
"	24.3.19		Ration train for HEUMAR. Rations - Men 12075. Animals 4573. 13th Hussars leave Div. above written Div. above 17th R. Div. from Div. received for men 25th.	
"	25.3.19		Ration train for HEUMAR. Rations - Men 12527. Animals 4470.	
"	26.3.19		Ration train from HEUMAR. Rations - Men 12237. Animals 4317.	

Army Form C. 2118.

WAR DIARY
INTELLIGENCE SUMMARY.
(Erase heading not required.)

Instructions regarding War Diaries and Intelligence Summaries are contained in F. S. Regs., Part II. and the Staff Manual respectively. Title pages will be prepared in manuscript.

Place	Date	Hour	Summary of Events and Information	Remarks and references to Appendices
MARTEN BURG Steenwerpoort (JOONDINE)	27.3.19		Rations drawn from HEUMAR Railhead – Men 12374 Animals 4529.	Dec. Q.M.S.
"	28.3.19		Rations drawn from HEUMAR – Men 11979 Animals 4525 (includes 390 Remount Horses) Dec. 123rd I.B. relieved 124th I.B. in left sector of Divisional front.	Dec. Q.M.F.
"	29.3.19		Rations drawn from HEUMAR – Men 11928 Animals 4644	Army Inst. Q.M.F.
"	30.3.19		Rations drawn from HEUMAR Railhead – Men 12432 Animals 4929. 1029 drawn rations	Army Inst. Q.M.F.
"	31.3.19		Rations drawn from HEUMAR Railhead – Men 12500 Animals 4266	Inst. Q.M.F.

WAR DIARY

INTELLIGENCE SUMMARY

(Erase heading not required.)

Army Form C. 2118.

Place	Date	Hour	Summary of Events and Information		Remarks and references to Appendices
MARIENBURG 5 Bayern(?) first COLOGNE	1.4.19		Ration drawn per Railtrans - Men 13015 Animals 4183.	Fine	[sig]
			41st Bde R.F.A (Newspaper(?) arrived by train Div) regan type Dec- Jan 31- Apl 3		
			On Apl 1-2 the 126th A.F.A Bde transferred to I Corps (Athens Division) he left on 2nd + 3rd		
			93rd Bde R.G.A transferred to I Corps VI Corps + both headquartered at the branch		
			51st B. Queens joined + being absorbed by 10th Queens. 52nd B. Queens joined + being absorbed by 11th Q s		
			53rd B. Queens joined + being absorbed by 2/4 Queens. 51st R. Fus. joined + being absorbed by 17th R. Fus.		
			52nd R. Fus. joined + being absorbed by 23rd R. Fus. 53rd R. Fus. joined + being absorbed by 26 R.F.		
			Approx. Men ration strength = 6932 (for above regiments)		
	2.4.19		Approx. Men ration strength of regiments = 7200	Fine	[sig]
			Ration drawn per Railtrans (note) - Men 14136 Animals 3516 (less understrength in receipt of Iron Ratn)		
	3.4.19		Rations drawn from Railhead (as noted) - Men 14858 Animals 4031 (less understrength in receipt of Iron Ratn)	Fine	[sig]
	4.4.19		Rations drawn from Railhead Men 15644 Animals 3885 (less understrength in receipt of Iron Ratn)	Fine	[sig]
	5.4.19		Rations drawn from Railhead. Men 16384 Animals 3809 (less understrength in receipt of Iron Ratn)	Fine	[sig]

Army Form C. 2118.

WAR DIARY
INTELLIGENCE SUMMARY.
(Erase heading not required.)

Instructions regarding War Diaries and Intelligence Summaries are contained in F. S. Regs., Part II. and the Staff Manual respectively. Title pages will be prepared in manuscript.

Place	Date	Hour	Summary of Events and Information	Weather	Remarks and references to Appendices
MARIENBURG 5 Bayenthal Gürtel Cologne	6.4.19		Rations drawn from Railhead Men 18779 (includes 1029 Indians) Animals 3789 (less under drawn rate)		
"	7.4.19		on acc/t of Snow Ration Rations drawn from Railhead Men 17700 Animals 3907 (less under drawn rate)	fine	
"			(from Ration)		
"	8.4.19		Rations drawn from Railhead Men 17284 Animals 3984	fine	
"	9.4.19		Rations drawn from Railhead Men 17403 Animals 3985	2 fine	
"	10.4.19		Rations drawn from Railhead Men 18192 Animals 4431	fine	
"	11.4.19		Rations drawn from Railhead Men 17567 Animals 4092	fine	
"	12.4.19		" Men 18143 Animals 4401	dull	
"	13.4.19		" Men 21643 (includes 1001 Indians) Animals 4076	wet	
"	14.4.19		" Men 17631 Animals 4081	fine	
"	15.4.19		" Men 18339 Animals 4110	fine	
"	16.4.19		" Men 18177 Animals 4242	wet	
"	17.4.19		" Men 18026 Animals 4184	fine	
"	18.4.19		" Men 18054 Animals 4197	fine	
"	19.4.19		" Men 17662 Animals 4224	fine	

Army Form C. 2118.

WAR DIARY
or
INTELLIGENCE SUMMARY.
(Erase heading not required.)

Instructions regarding War Diaries and Intelligence Summaries are contained in F. S. Regs., Part II. and the Staff Manual respectively. Title pages will be prepared in manuscript.

S.S.O.
LONDON DIVISION.

Place	Date	Hour	Summary of Events and Information	Remarks and references to Appendices
MARIENBURG 5 Bayerthal Strasse COLOGNE	20.4.19		Rations drawn from Railhead HEUMAR MEN 18474 includes 1001 Indian Rations Animals 4334	P.W.
	21.4.19		Rations drawn from Railhead HEUMAR MEN 17263 Animals 4196	P.W.
	22.4.19		Rations drawn from Railhead HEUMAR MEN 19334 Animals 4216	P.W.
	23.4.19		Rations drawn from Railhead HEUMAR MEN 17238 Animals 4279	P.W.
	24.4.19		Rations drawn from Railhead HEUMAR MEN 16993 Animals 4281	P.W.
	25.4.19		Rations drawn for HEUMAR Railhead - Men 16802 Animals 4239	P.W.
	26.4.19		Rations drawn for HEUMAR Railhead - Men 16831 Animals 4333	P.W.
	27.4.19		Rations drawn for HEUMAR Railhead - Men 16534 Animals 4303 also rations for 997 Indian	P.W.
	28.4.19		Rations drawn for HEUMAR Railhead - Men 17598 Animals 4395	P.W.
	29.4.19		Rations drawn for HEUMAR Railhead - Men 17113 Animals 4313	P.W.
	30.4.19		Rations drawn for Heumar Railhead - Men 17134 Animals 4279	P.W.

MAJOR
A. & S.O. LONDON DIVISION

www.ingramcontent.com/pod-product-compliance
Lightning Source LLC
Chambersburg PA
CBHW081550160426
43191CB00011B/1887